Advance Praise

"Now more than ever, educators need to feel encouraged and empowered to teach literature that reflects what is happening in the world today, that acknowledges and reckons with the past, and that enlivens hope for an equitable and just future. *Literature and the New Culture Wars* is the book that honors and makes visible those educators doing this necessary work."

—**Marcelle Haddix,** Associate Provost for Strategic Initiatives, Syracuse University

"Finding the vocabulary—neither offensive nor defensive—to confront book challenges has never been more difficult than today. Enter Deborah Appleman. With extraordinary candor, she models the kind of intellectual rigor that teachers and school leaders need to employ when complaints converge from both the right and the left. You need this book and need it now."

—**Carol Jago,** High school English teacher, past president of the National Council of Teachers of English, and author of *The Book in Question: Why and How Reading Is in Crisis*

"If I could buy just one book for every English teacher in America at this time, it would this one. Everything Deborah Appleman has written and thought about in the past would seem to have been in preparation for this moment in time, so that she would be ready to write this book about our profession, our country, and our place as English teachers in these difficult and, at times, even dangerous conversations. Appleman brings us all, whatever our perspective or place on the political spectrum, to the table and helps us have the conversation we so badly need to have about our work, our schools, our communities, and our country. The fact that she manages to also fit in, at the end of each chapter, practical suggestions about how to apply the ideas she discusses to our own classrooms and curriculum makes this book all the more of a blessing, for so often we are often left with the question, after discussing many of these issues for the umpteenth time with colleagues or reading such a book, 'Yes, but what should I *do* in my classroom tomorrow?' Drawing on her remarkable career as a classroom teacher, scholar, literacy leader, activist, and author, Deborah Appleman shows us the way forward that I have been looking for and am so grateful to find in this book."

—**Jim Burke,** Middle College High School,
San Mateo, CA, and author of *The English Teacher's Companion* (Heinemann) and *Uncharted Territory* (W. W. Norton)

"Deborah Appleman is one of the legendary mentors of our profession. Her latest and perhaps most courageous book arrives at the right moment to rescue literary education in American schools from the anti-literate, parochial, and self-righteous censors from across the political spectrum, who don't begin to understand that the function of literature is to awaken our sense of outrage and empathy, trouble our platitudes, and arouse us to moral action."

—**Sheridan Blau, PhD,** Professor of Practice in the Teaching of English, Teachers College, Columbia University

"Appleman brings a wealth of knowledge as an academic, instructor, researcher, teacher, and social activist to her writing about the current cultural wars focused on book banning, canonical texts, #MeToo, and trigger warnings. She includes definitions of terms and contextualizes their use and potential for pedagogical decision-making. She also deconstructs ill-conceived narratives by describing how tensions within politics and society can affect the teaching of literature. Eschewing oppositional binaries, she encourages teachers and instructors to draw upon academic freedom in support of students' agency, emerging critical consciousnesses, and personal freedoms. Her book is inspired by a variety of authors, historians, scholars, and teachers.

This book seeks to provide a balanced discussion of why, and how, past and contemporary manifestations of historical, political, and social concerns can affect the teaching of literature. Appleman supports addressing and explicating the lack of diversity, equity, and inclusion in heteronormative, white-centric, canonical literature, and mentions the voiced and unvoiced discomfort expressed by some readers and teachers who wish to retain the status quo. The decentering of whiteness and the unlearning of white supremacy requires centering BIPOC cultures, experiences, histories, languages, and racial/ethnic communities in literature as worthy and valuable. Appleman also provides alternative instructional approaches and strategies to use in classrooms."

—**Arlette Ingram Willis,** professor, University of Illinois

LITERATURE *and the*

NEW CULTURE WARS

LITERATURE *and the*

NEW CULTURE WARS

TRIGGERS, CANCEL CULTURE,

AND THE TEACHER'S DILEMMA

Deborah Appleman

W. W. NORTON & COMPANY
Independent Publishers Since 1923

This work is intended as a general information resource for educators. It is not a substitute for appropriate professional education or training. Standards of clinical practice and protocol change over time, and no technique or recommendation is guaranteed to be effective in all circumstances.

As of press time, the URLs displayed in this book link or refer to existing websites. The publisher is not responsible for, and should not be deemed to endorse or recommend, any website other than its own or any content available on the Internet or elsewhere, including, without limitation, any app, website, blog page, or information page, that the publisher did not create. The author also is not responsible for any material that the author did not create.

Stuck In The Middle With You
Words and Music by Gerry Rafferty and Joe Egan
Copyright © 1973; Renewed 2005 Stage Three Music (Catalogues) Limited and Baby Bun Music Ltd.
All Rights for Stage Three Music (Catalogues) Limited Administered by BMG Rights Management (US) LLC
All Rights Reserved   Used by Permission
Reprinted by Permission of Hal Leonard LLC

Excerpt(s) from BREAKING BREAD WITH THE DEAD: A READER'S GUIDE TO A MORE TRANQUIL MIND by Alan Jacobs, copyright © 2020 by Alan Jacobs. Used by permission of Penguin Books, an imprint of Penguin Publishing Group, a division of Penguin Random House LLC. All rights reserved.

For Mike Rose, whose memory is a blessing

CONTENTS

ACKNOWLEDGMENTS

First and foremost, thank you to Carol Chambers Collins, who saw the possibilities of this book before I did.

Thank you to the high school teachers who continue to inspire and to push me, especially the ELA teachers at South High School and Henry High School in Minneapolis, Minnesota. You know who you are!

Thank you to John Schmit, whose patience and wisdom tempers me at every turn.

Thank you to Jeffrey Snyder and Amna Khalid, whose work encouraged my thinking.

Thank you to Tonja Clay, whose combination of kindness and efficiency is unbeatable.

Thank you to Jim Marshall, Michael Smith, and Jeff Wilhelm for believing in me all these years. You made me feel smarter than I am.

Thank you to David Rathbun for curating and sharing the relevant and the outrageous.

A very special thank you to Trina Eichel for her expert editing and thoughtful reading.

Thank you to Richard Beach and the late James Mackey, who sent me on my way.

Thank you, posthumously, to the late, great Mike Rose. Let us honor his legacy by teaching with empathy and writing with humility.

LITERATURE *and the*

NEW CULTURE WARS

CHAPTER 1

"Clowns to the Left of Me, Jokers to the Right"

Clowns to the left of me!
Jokers to the right!
Here I am stuck in the middle with you.

—STEALERS WHEEL,
"STUCK IN THE MIDDLE WITH YOU"

I hate it when I find myself agreeing with people with whom I usually disagree. When I am in alignment with people whose positions I generally find unacceptable, I begin to question my own judgment as well as my understanding of the issues at hand. This kind of dissonance may not always be a bad thing, but it is disconcerting, to say the least. The current debate on what literature is acceptable to read in our nation's classrooms as well as the ubiquitous and chilling nature of trigger warnings and cancel culture have indeed made strange bedfellows for me. From a theoretical perspective, I find myself in reluctant agreement with those critics who have long insisted on separating writers from their works, a kind of New Critical stance I have previously summarily rejected (Appleman, 2015). As a high school teacher and an English education professor, I opposed the insistence on singular meanings, the purposeful separation of the author from the text, and the dismissal of the importance of readers' affective responses. Yet now, from a pedagogical perspective, I am astonished to find myself arguing in favor of retaining some canonical texts alongside those conservative voices that have maddeningly resisted attempts to diversify the secondary literature curriculum. From a political perspective, I find myself a liberal misfit surrounded by those who label anything seemingly progressive as too woke when it comes to current literary challenges in the classroom.

How did this happen? How could I, a self-proclaimed progressive educator committed to centering previously underrepresented literary voices and amplifying the perspectives and lived experiences of my increasingly diverse student population, possibly find myself agreeing with those who consistently complain about some of the excesses that characterize the current political moment? I believe in diversifying the literature curriculum. I believe that literature should function as both "windows and mirrors" (Sims Bishop, 1990) for all of our students, reflecting their lived experiences. I also believe that students should be taught to read and resist the ideology inscribed in both texts and worlds (Appleman, 2015). So why am I resisting some of the most significant gestures of this new movement for social justice and equality, gestures that include cancel culture, trigger warnings, and the removal of texts from the literature curriculum in both secondary and postsecondary classrooms?

The political challenges of teaching literature in the 2020s come, interestingly enough, from both conservative and liberal fronts. From the right, the Common Core state standards movement has sadly reduced the reading of literature into hard-boiled recitations of text-based facts, completely eschewing the affective and aesthetic dimensions of literature. Concomitant with the Common Core movement has been an increase in the role of nonfiction and informational texts in the literature curriculum. While learning to read and decode such texts are clearly valuable skills, the richness of literature cannot be replaced with a diet of dry and static informational texts. Censorship used to be the province of the right, of social conservatives. Books were censored because they included too much sex or vulgar language or, in recent times, books that had gay or trans identity themes. Also from the conservative spectrum are the usual objections based on perceived standards of appropriateness for classroom consumption, including obscenity, explicit sex, portrayals of LGBTQ characters and relationships, alcohol and substance abuse, and other topics.

These kinds of efforts of censorship are not new. Yet it is not only the pressure from the right that challenges and politicizes the teaching of literature in the 21st century. In classrooms all over the country, from elementary to graduate school, other movements now threaten the teaching of literature. Despite my ardent support of the need to protect the vulnerable and the victimized, I do have concerns about the ways in which trigger warnings, cancel culture, and the #MeToo movement have reshaped the politics of teaching literature. Additionally, cleansing the curriculum of any potentially offensive language or character portrayals has had a significant influence on what does and does not get taught. This introductory chapter will outline the current debates and discuss the ramifications of those debates on the teaching of literature in secondary and postsecondary classrooms. It will also preview some possible approaches to addressing the concerns raised by those objecting to the content of certain texts on a variety of grounds while preserving the pedagogical autonomy of teachers and the opportunity for students to experience challenging and troublesome texts.

Over the past few decades, there have been many disconcerting challenges to texts in both the university and high school literary canon, but a recent challenge hit especially close to home. The school where decades ago I began my high school teaching career just announced that they were going to temporarily pause the teaching of John Steinbeck's *Of Mice and Men*, which had been assigned to ninth-grade language arts students. *Of Mice and Men*, a book about itinerant migrant workers that is typically considered an American classic, has been frequently challenged and has been banned at numerous schools, whose administrators cite its profanity and racial slurs as unacceptable. The letter announcing the pause cited recent "communication from families and staff expressing concerns about racist stereotypes and slurs used in the novel" (Verges, 2020).

This incident was not merely a pedagogical or philosophical jolt for me; it was personal. I began my career in that school teaching *Of Mice and Men*. In fact, I had battled for the right to teach the book with a senior faculty member who believed it "belonged" to her advanced English classes. I fought hard to be able to teach the book with my tracked section of struggling readers. It was one of the few pieces of bona fide American literature that they could actually read easily and comprehend. The readability and the length of the book made it accessible to students of all ability levels.

Ironically, I taught the novel because I thought it offered significant lessons about the diversity of humanity. Rather than essentializing or demeaning marginalized groups, I thought the novel challenged the reader to consider how a dominant culture uses and abuses defenseless others. For example, each one of the characters is a member of some marginalized group, through race (Crooks), gender (Curley's wife), age (Candy), and limited physical (Candy) and cognitive (Lenny) abilities. Each of these empathetically drawn characters is oppressed and mistreated by a single ruling force (Curley), a stand-in for a cruel capitalistic system, a heartless hegemonic machine that takes advantage of its workers. The characters come together bonded by their common humanity, vulnerability, and their marginalization, emulating the collective synergy of the migrant workers Steinbeck found so captivating. The strongly drawn and robust characters draw empathy from adolescent readers. Moral and ethical issues are presented not didactically, but within a narrative frame. There is a lot to be learned by reading about characters like this.

Challenging *Of Mice and Men* is nothing new. It is among the most challenged books of the last few decades. From 2000 to 2009, it ranked among the top ten most challenged books in America, and it sits at number 8 on the American Library Association's list of all-time most challenged books. Challenges have included complaints about "profanity," "morbid and depressing themes," and the author's alleged "anti-business attitude." Other complaints have accused the book of being demeaning and derogatory to several marginalized populations, including African Americans, women, and the developmentally disabled. As with other novels that have been challenged, one issue is the language. Steinbeck, as well as his advocates, asserted that his intention was to create an accurate portrayal of the people in central California. That meant writing dialogue that sounded the way real people talked, with profanity, slurs, and slang. In fact, the language in the book is the main reason it has been challenged so much. The n-word appears nine times in the book.

A couple of decades later, the challenges to the novel have been renewed, another casualty of the literary cancel culture this book will address. This latest assault on the novel seems to belong to a larger movement, markedly different in its ideological bent. According to this movement, the literature curriculum needs to be purged of works that offend. There are whole movements dedicated to doing just that—removing texts that have reductive or offensive portrayals of characters, centering works by authors of color and other underrepresented groups, refraining from teaching works that perpetuate the dominant culture, or reading texts to simply expose their flawed ideologies.

In a stunningly revealing explanation that goes to the heart of the problems with the assumptions about why we read literature and about the role certain texts may have in a student's literary education, a spokesperson for the school district that paused the teaching of *Of Mice and Men* stated that rather than teaching the novel, there are other curricular materials that can "address the *skills* the novel is supposed to teach. Students have been reassigned a series of short stories that teach the same skills," the school said (Verges, 2020). To be fair, in this particular case, the school district said it was pausing, not necessarily permanently abandoning the teaching of the novel. Rather, according to the school district's letter, the goal of suspending the lessons was to "determine how the content of this novel was addressed during the curriculum so we could respond to the concerns in a meaningful and informed manner" (Verges, 2020). The implication is that the novel only serves to deliver a discrete and articulated set of skills, skills that are easily transferable from one literary text (e.g., piece of curricular material) to another. Although the teaching of literacy skills is clearly important, the teaching of literature is about much more than delivering skills. Reading literature has larger purposes, including an invitation to reflect on oneself and one's culture, developing empathy and understanding of others, and developing aesthetic sensibilities, among other goals. Additionally, given their varied rhetorical styles, historical and geographical contexts, and artistic as well as social purposes, novels are not easily interchangeable with other works of fiction—including other novels.

This is a very different argument than proposing that different novels are considered to offer students equally valuable literary experiences. This statement reveals a complete lack of understanding of the value and purposes of literature, values that, as I will continue to argue throughout this book, are being undermined by this current movement of literary cancel culture. This is not to say that this book, *Of Mice and Men*, in itself is the topic. I am not making a canonical argument here. I am not arguing on behalf of particular books; I am arguing to preserve the importance of literary reading.

Literary reading, to invoke Louise Rosenblatt (1938), is both an efferent and an aesthetic experience. Put another way, literature helps us learn to think and encourages us to feel. Literature provides windows into the lives and perspectives of others and mirrors into our own experiences. Literature helps us to understand what it means to be human. Through literature, we will be both awed by the beauty and confronted with the complexity of the human condition. Therefore, through literature we will confront some ugly truths about humankind, truths that should not be avoided. The power of literature should not be removed by cancellation or censure or be blunted by trigger warnings.

In an article that explores whether the reading of literature makes us more human, Karen Swallow Prior (2013) testifies to the power of literature to help shape who we are:

> The books I have read over a lifetime have shaped my worldview, my beliefs, and my life as much as anything else. From *Great Expectations* I learned the power the stories we tell ourselves have to do either harm and good, to ourselves and to others; from *Death of a Salesman* I learned the dangers of a corrupt version of

the American Dream; from *Madame Bovary,* I learned
to embrace the real world rather than escaping into
flights of fancy; from *Gulliver's Travels* I learned the
profound limitations of my own finite perspective;
and from *Jane Eyre* I learned how to be myself. These
weren't mere intellectual or moral lessons, although
they certainly may have begun as such. Rather, the
stories from these books and so many others became
part of my life story and then, gradually, part of my
very soul. (para. 9)

Each literary work, whether classic or contemporary,
reveals a universe of thought, of characters, and of perspectives and settings that can be both jarring and unsettling. While I wholeheartedly believe in the value of
centering new and diverse voices into the curriculum, it's
important that they are welcomed for their own merit.
Enacting a restricted sensibility will make it even less
likely that bold and contemporary literary texts will be
embraced.

I believe that we teachers, like physicians, have our
own version of the Hippocratic oath: "First do no harm."
If there are elements of a particular text that cause distress among student readers, its place in the curriculum

needs to be reconsidered. Distress is different from discomfort. In fact, don't we read not to avoid discomfort, but to experience it? As Kafka (1959) wrote:

> I think we ought to read only the kind of books that wound or stab us. If the book we're reading doesn't wake us up with a blow to the head, what are we reading for? So that it will make us happy, as you write? Good Lord, we would be happy precisely if we had no books, and the kind of books that make us happy are the kind we could write ourselves if we had to. But we need books that affect us like a disaster, that grieve us deeply, like the death of someone we loved more than ourselves, like being banished into forests far from everyone, like a suicide. A book must be the axe for the frozen sea within us. That is my belief. (p. 16)

If we remove all literary works with texture, complexity, and realism, what will remain for our students? A rote curriculum completely devoid of the opportunity to confront and discuss real world issues in a safe space? A list of texts that meet students exactly where they are, in terms of beliefs, experience, and perspective? A menu of readings that does not provoke, disrupt, or challenge? Society in general and educators in particular will fail students miserably if we let that happen.

In many of the literary works currently under assault, as with *Of Mice and Men*, there are indeed issues of representation and vocabulary, but they are issues that are both discussable and profitable to explore. Their problematic dimensions provide reasons why they should continue to be taught; not reasons why they should be banished. Using these challenged texts, we can invite readers to think through the questions of the dominant narrative and think about whose voices are represented and about how certain groups of people are portrayed and by whom. We can raise issues of authority, representation, and authenticity. We can raise questions of ideology through various theoretical perspectives, as I describe in *Critical Encounters in Secondary English: Teaching Literary Theory to Adolescents* (Appleman, 2015). Interpreting literary texts through theoretical perspectives such as gender criticism, postcolonial theory, Marxist literary theory, deconstruction, formalism, structuralism, and reader response, for example, can become a center of literary inquiry. We can lay bare inequalities and issues of racism and sexism not by refusing to teach the offending texts, but by doing the opposite: actually teaching them.

Herein lies the challenge. Teachers of literary texts need to find some way to strike a balance between excluding texts that are demeaning, offensive, and downright harmful and retaining texts that include some problematic elements such as language, dialogue, and representation but have important value—aesthetically, historically, developmentally, and curricularly. We also need to think about the differences between simply excluding a potentially troublesome text from the curriculum and thinking about how it can be taught, troubled, and even disrupted. A central tenet of this book is this: rather than omitting troublesome texts reflexively from the curriculum, we should consider how we can offer them in the classroom, not as a way of reproducing the troublesome content therein but as a way of teaching students and other readers to resist that troublesome content by understanding and examining the source of it.

A significant issue here is what seems to be an attempt to remove some of the grittier aspects of life from the literature curriculum and from the classroom so that students will not be exposed to them or troubled by them. Yet part of the function of literature is to provide a mirror for certain aspects of life. This argument holds true for our case in question, *Of Mice and Men*. In writing the novel, Steinbeck tried to capture a particular group of people in a particular setting with particular issues. He actually spent time working with migrant workers to capture the nuances of their lives. He didn't make them up; they existed. Whether he exaggerated certain character traits for effect may be debated, but he tried to ground his portrayal realistically in order to represent them truthfully. His obligation as a writer, then—and, we could argue, one of the primary obligations of all writers—was to represent reality. Reality is ugly. It is full of complexities and thorny moral dilemmas. Part of the function of literature is to present that ugliness as well as those dilemmas.

The case of *Of Mice and Men* raises several questions about whether it might be possible to profitably teach troublesome texts by troubling them, rather than eliminating them. There are several ways to do this, which is what Chapters 4 and 5 will explore in greater detail. For example, this novel allows us to invoke a historical context that focuses on itinerant migrant workers and locates both the language and character portrayals within a particular historical and geographical context.

Considering the author's intent, perspective, and ideology to the extent that we do is also important. What is the social project or perspective of their work and to what extent is the author him or herself engaged in some of the issues or social inequities that are brought forward by the text? For example, throughout his life, John Steinbeck remained a champion of the downtrodden and oppressed. In fact, Tom Joad's speech near the end of *The Grapes of Wrath* might have been spoken by Steinbeck himself:

> I'll be all aroun' in the dark. I'll be ever'where—wherever you look. Wherever they's a fight so hungry people can eat, I'll be there. Wherever they's a cop beaten up a guy, I'll be there . . . . I'll be in the way guys yell when they're mad an'—I'll be in the way kids laugh when they're hungry and they know supper's ready. An' when our folks eat the stuff they raise an' live in the houses they build—why, I'll be there. (p. 419)

Steinbeck felt that his portrayal of characters, now considered to be problematic, even offensive, was a way not of oppressing them but of potentially working against that oppression by offering a sympathetic (yes, sympathetic) portrait of marginalized migrant workers that would make a wider audience more aware of their circumstances.

Another way to trouble or question troubling texts is to use a variety of critical lenses or literary theories to disrupt a normative reading of the texts and to highlight certain elements of the text. For example, a gender lens highlights how Curley's wife is treated. Even her lack of a proper name is fodder for a discussion about the marginalization and objectification of women in the novel, as is her treatment by Curley and all the other characters. It also brings into focus some intentionality on Steinbeck's part. Was he so pressed for time, I used to ask my high school students, that he couldn't think of a name for her? Of course not! He is asking us to note how she is treated. Similarly, a use of a Marxist or class lens helps us see the degree to which the workers are symbolic stand-ins for the downtrodden while Curley himself is a manifestation of the cruelty, coldness, and corruption of the ruling class. Steinbeck is inviting us to consider these dynamics and to be as outraged as he was. To ban the novel is to ban Steinbeck's invitation for us to engage with and empathize with these characters.

Then there is the fact that the n-word appears nine times in the novel. Although the use of this hideous word is highly problematic, especially within the context of our current racial reckoning, the use of the word itself may not completely or automatically preclude the teaching of this or other novels for whom it has been a deal breaker, for example, *To Kill a Mockingbird* or *Adventures of Huckleberry Finn*. Rather than not teach the novel at all, many teachers have followed the advice presented by seasoned teachers such as Michelle Kenney (2014) in a recent *Rethinking Schools* article and choose to teach about the word before embarking on reading a piece of literature that contains it. The whole notion of disrupting texts is not to banish them, but to trouble them. Therein lie the larger lessons of social justice.

Conclusion

Nearly thirty years ago, Arthur Applebee (1993) presciently admonished teachers and scholars to reconsider both the philosophy and the praxis of the teaching of literature. In today's particularly fraught political times, it seems even more important to do so. All of the cherished bedrocks of our democracy are imperiled, from freedom of expression, to the future of a free and independent press, to the promise of safety and dignity for all. So, too, is the pursuit of literature instruction, a cherished intellectual and affective activity, one that can ensure the future of a well-informed citizenry as well as the opportunity for all of our students to have literate lives.

We need to confront the challenges that are faced by teachers of literature at both the secondary and postsecondary level. These challenges include a culture that cancels out authors and bans books, the institutionalization of compulsory trigger warnings in the literature classroom, and the censorship of language and other aspects of literary texts that are deemed culturally insensitive but may actually help build students' understanding of diversity and difference. In the chapters that follow, this book examines these challenges and argues that rather than banish these troubled texts from our classrooms, they should continue to be taught, not by ignoring the controversies they invoke, but by inviting them into our classrooms and encouraging our students to trouble them.

CHAPTER 2

Authors in Peril: Cancel Culture and #MeToo

A word is dead when it is said, some say.
I say, it just begins to live that day.

—EMILY DICKINSON

I confess: I am a Sherman Alexie fan. Yes, still. Before you stop reading in disgust, please let me explain. As a high school English teacher in an urban school, I strove to offer literature of diverse authors. I believe strongly in the windows and mirrors approach to teaching literature, a perspective that asserts that literature needs to be both a window that gives us insight into the realities of others and a mirror that reflects our own reality. As I gazed at my diverse class, I noticed the raised hand of a Native student I will call Pine. She told me that ever since she learned to read she had been waiting to read something written by a Native American author. I told her that her wait was finally over. I was about to introduce her to Sherman Alexie. With the wit and irrepressible energy found in the stories of *The Lone Ranger and Tonto Fistfight in Heaven,* Alexie did not disappoint Pine. When the class was over, Pine attached a carefully written note to her course evaluation: "Thank you for teaching Sherman Alexie. My understanding of the world of literature and how I fit into it is forever changed."

In addition to tens of thousands of adolescents who have profited both intellectually and psychologically from reading Alexie's writing, I came to treasure his work in two other contexts. As a college professor, I found the inclusion of Alexie's work in our Introduction to American Studies class to be of paramount importance. His piece "What You Pawn I Will Redeem" (2003) spoke eloquently to some of the major themes of the course in particular and to American studies in general—themes like cultural homelessness, redemption, identity, vanishing and stolen Native American culture, ethnic heritage, displacement, and stereotyping. I can think of no piece of writing that does quite the same work in the same way. His most recent book, about his mother's passing, *You Don't Have to Say You Love Me,* was a genre-defying literary masterpiece that spoke to me eloquently as I grieved my own mother's death. Alexie was on tour for this book when, as part of the #MeToo movement, he was publicly accused by multiple women of sexual harassment and exploitation. Suffering exhaustion, depression, and relentless public scorn from the literary community, he was forced to abruptly quit the book tour and cancel all speaking engagements, including a much-heralded appearance at the Annual Convention of the National Council of Teachers of English.

Since his scandal broke, Alexie's books have been stripped of previous literary awards, removed from library shelves, and canceled in secondary literature curricula. He has become a pariah, and some might argue deservedly so. Are his books any less brilliant now that the scandal has broken? Is his work any less important? Is the value of his writing diminished by his allegedly reprehensible personal behavior? I have been urged to stop fussing about this, warned that my stubborn allegiance to the worth of his work impugns my liberal feminist credentials. My teacher friends have encouraged me to simply replace him with other texts by Native American writers, such as the highly praised *There, There* by Tommy Orange. Or, perhaps, replace Alexie's work with the work of some of the women writers he allegedly exploited. Perhaps that would be a kind of literary and social justice.

For me, there is no simple solution to this issue. I do not believe that writers and their work are interchangeable merely because they belong to the same general category. I am not arguing for a new reified canon, or, for that matter, for an old one. The notion that texts and writers do equivalent work because of superficial similarities is, in my opinion, just plain wrong and reductive. Second, I can't justify denying my students Alexie's work because of the accusations of sexual misconduct that surround him. Who are we punishing by withholding his work? Some have made an economic argument, that we are punishing him by ensuring that he won't be able to profit from his work. These colleagues even go as far as to make a distinction between the rules of cancel culture for living authors and the rules of cancel culture for dead authors. Ultimately, I think those who would be punished by canceling Alexie's work are the readers, like my student, Pine, who would be denied the benefit of his writing.

I do not want to understate the outrage that has been felt by the literary community about Sherman Alexie's alleged transgressions. Still, the quality of the work remains, and its value as literature has not changed, even if the reputation of the author has. How far are we willing to go to rid the curriculum of anyone whose behavior is problematic regardless of the quality of their work?

This type of censure is a new variation on an old theme of banning books. The difference is that this canceling is about the authors themselves, not necessarily about their work. It belongs much more clearly to a relatively recent, 20th-century phenomenon: cancel culture. According to the Lone Star Research Group (2021),

> the term "Cancel Culture" has been used in the last four to five years to encompass not only materials such as books but also people and their actions. Dr. Tina Sikka defines cancel culture as the "act of publicly shaming someone for a perceived or substantive social transgression that hasn't been adequately addressed through traditional channels." (para. 1)

In the arena of literary studies, some literature has come under fire because the work of particular authors has been reappraised due to recent and unprecedented scrutiny into their personal lives. This has affected the appraisal of both historical and contemporary figures, who, after serious allegations of sexual misconduct, have been caught up in the #MeToo movement. It has become a politically incorrect and pedagogically inappropriate choice for some to teach Sherman Alexie, or Junot Díaz, or David Foster Wallace. Even the Holocaust survivor and author of *Night*, Elie Wiesel, has been shunned by the movement. Not only has Alexie's work been removed from libraries and classrooms all over the country, but also the quality of his once widely praised work has undergone a reappraisal. What should we do in the case of Sherman Alexie? It's a question we must all ask ourselves. We should be prepared to understand that there are different answers to that question.

These developments make left-leaning scholars strange bedfellows with more conservatively aligned New Critics, such as I. A. Richards. We may again need to evaluate the relative value of literature as it exists apart from the author; for me, both as a teacher and as a scholar of literary study, the proponents of the New Critical movement were the theoretical opposition. Their insistence on decontextualized literary study devoid of both historical and biographical background contexts baffled me. Even more baffling was their insistence that the predispositions and responses of the reader were not relevant to the literary experience, or were, as I. A. Richards (1929) deemed them, a "mnemonic irrelevance."

The practice of divorcing the author from the text seemed ridiculous to me, one that would rob readers of a fruitful interpretive vein to mine. Now, unexpectedly and ironically, I find myself pleading for that kind of aesthetic divide. I want to be able to access the work of an important artist regardless of his or her personal choices or transgressions. To whose code of appropriate moral behavior should we adhere? Whose art, music, writing, or film would we be left with if we applied a litmus test of morality to some of our most revered artists? Whose art would remain?

Of course, artistic genius should not excuse sexual misconduct, and those who engage in inappropriate behavior need to be held accountable. However, are we as a culture really prepared to articulate and then agree upon and consistently reinforce a set of standards of moral behavior for writers and other artists? Do we have the right to do that? Is there a difference between making people accountable for their behavior in ways that are serious yet somehow separated from the consumption of their art, or is it impossible to do so? These are questions that all educators should ask themselves before banishing a book to the dust pile.

There are many reasons why an author might be canceled by contemporary cultural critics. The case of Sherman Alexie is a primary example of authors who have been canceled because of allegations of sexual harassment or misconduct. There are other reasons as well. J. K. Rowling, author of the beloved Harry Potter series, was canceled because of a tweet that was considered transphobic. Because Rowling has refused to take back her tweet, citing not only free speech but a sense that she expressed a belief that might have been subsequently misconstrued, her banishment or ostracizing has been maintained. Because of a perceived abhorrent social attitude, should her books—which have done more than most others to turn young people into readers—be removed from the possibility of becoming part of young people's reading lives? According to trans writer Rori Porter (2019), "Sometimes cancel culture is necessary to lessen the reach of people who ought not to be reaching the minds of children." This controversy exemplifies the difficulty of separating an author from his or her work, given the harm that transphobic attitudes cause, especially to the young people Rowling's books had previously reached.

Another type of canceling is when the portrayal in a text is deemed to be inauthentic. Much has been made recently of the kerfuffle involving the novel *American Dirt* by Jeanine Cummins (2019). First hailed with rapturous praise and chosen for Oprah's Book Club, the book was later excoriated for cultural appropriation and stereotyping, raising the question of who gets to tell whose story. There was outrage from some members of the Latinx community; critics actually rewrote their initially positive reviews of the book; and her publisher, Flatiron, canceled the book tour, citing "concerns about safety" and "specific threats to booksellers and the author." As Rebecca Alter (2020) explains, "One of the more common knocks is that the book engages in 'brownface,' incorporating a nominally Mexican perspective that was written by a woman who—as recently as 2016—identified as 'white.'" The book and the author were canceled not only because of a sense of cultural appropriation—that is, who should have been able to tell the story—but also because of the stereotypical and inaccurate way in which the characters were portrayed. In her essay titled "Pendeja, You Ain't Steinbeck: My Bronca With Fake-Ass Social Justice Literature," Myriam Gurba (2019) criticizes *American Dirt* for its reliance on "overly ripe" Mexican stereotypes, for its portrayal of characters who are either comically evil or angelically good, for the inaccurate Spanish sprinkled in italics throughout the text, and for the "white gaze" of the authorial perspective.

This incident raised important larger questions that extend well beyond the case of *American Dirt*. Who gets to tell whose story? Don't all fiction writers, to a certain extent, inhabit other perspectives? Is it only when racial boundaries are crossed or there is some ambiguity about the author's background that it becomes an issue? Some might argue Cummins brought it on herself when she,

citing her Puerto Rican grandmother, wished that "someone browner than herself" (p. 348) could tell the story. By
clumsily acknowledging the question of who gets to tell
the story, Cummins seemed to make the situation worse
by attempting to assert some ethnic authenticity that was
questionable at best and manipulative at worst.

Recently, a few young adult authors have been canceled, not for any potentially questionable material in
their books but for other reasons that have to do with canceling out the author rather than the book. Jessica Cluess,
author of the wildly popular young adult *Kingdom of Fire*
series, was canceled after writing a tweet that defended
classic literature such as *The Scarlet Letter*. Unfortunately,
in her defense of the classics, she directly and vehemently
disparaged Lorena German, an educator and cofounder
of the #DisruptTexts movement. Cluess's language and
attitude were indeed inappropriate, but the response to
her now-deleted tweets was swift, fierce, and relentless.
According to Spencer Baculi, after she was accused of
being a racist, her agent dropped her as a client, and thousands of English teachers rose to the defense of German
and have stopped teaching Cluess's books (Baculi, 2020).

There have also been some prepublication cancellations that have been spectacular in their swiftness. In
"How a Twitter Mob Derailed an Immigrant Author's

Budding Career," (2019) Jesse Singal explains how she canceled her own lucrative three-book deal through pressure. The work of emerging writer Amelie Wen Zhao was ravaged on a social media community called YA Twitter. YA Twitter is comprised of adolescent readers, YA authors, and some critics as well. As Kat Rosenfield (2017) wrote, "Young-adult books are being targeted in intense social media callouts, draggings, and pile-ons—sometimes before anybody's even read them." Zhao was accused of racial insensitivity, indeed racism, due in large part to the role that both chattel slavery and color blindness allegedly played in her book, although many of the people who were complaining about it had actually never read it.

This is a powerful portent of the potential effects of cancel culture: It is not only the consumption of literary works, but the very production of literary works, of art itself, that can be canceled by what Jesse Singal has called "righteous disciplinarians" (2019, p. 10). Kosoko Jackson, a black and queer YA author, noted by Katy Waldman (2019) as "exactly the type of voice that many people want to lift up," withdrew the publication of his much anticipated novel *A Place for Wolves* after a Twitter eruption berating his portrayal of Muslims and the Kosovo War. Similarly, Laurie Forest's YA fantasy debut,

"The Black Witch," became the object of intense scrutiny weeks before its publication "after detractors slammed it as a white-savior tale" (Waldman, 2019). Kat Rosenfield's 2017 *New York Magazine* piece, "The Toxic Drama of YA Twitter," which centered on the "Black Witch" outcry, revealed that many of Forest's fiercest critics had not read her novel, and others conflated the perspectives of racist characters with that of the author herself.

Interestingly, much of the outcry is due to either critics not reading the book itself, or in the case of Laurie Forest, conflating the words and attitudes of a character with the words and attitudes of the author. This points not only to the increasingly influential presence of what commentator Anne Applebaum has labeled "Twitter mob mentality" (Applebaum, 2021), but also to a fundamental misreading of texts. For a teacher of literature, these controversies point to a colossal literary miseducation that is equally alarming. It is one thing to mount a considered critique about a literary text that one has read; it's another to do so without either having read the text, or worse, not understanding some of the basic premises of how fiction works.

Writers Fighting Back

This proliferation of the pushback in cancel culture has

created distress not just for readers and educators, but for many writers as well. In a now oft-cited document, 150 writers, scholars, journalists, and artists wrote an open letter published in *Harper's Magazine* (2020). The writers decried what they perceived to be a threat to the possibility of open debate and discussion:

> The free exchange of information and ideas, the life-blood of a liberal society, is daily becoming more constricted. While we have come to expect this on the radical right, censoriousness is also spreading more widely in our culture: an intolerance of opposing views, a vogue for public shaming and ostracism, and the tendency to dissolve complex policy issues in a blinding moral certainty. . . . Editors are fired for running controversial pieces; books are withdrawn for alleged inauthenticity; journalists are barred from writing on certain topics; professors are investigated for quoting works of literature in class; a researcher is fired for circulating a peer-reviewed academic study; and the heads of organizations are ousted for what are sometimes just clumsy mistakes. Whatever the arguments around each particular incident, the result has been to steadily narrow the boundaries of what can be said without the threat of reprisal. We

are already paying the price in greater risk aversion among writers, artists, and journalists who fear for their livelihoods if they depart from the consensus, or even lack sufficient zeal in agreement. (para. 2)

These writers, many if not most of whom are considered left-leaning, find themselves in the uncomfortably dissonant location I described in the opening chapter. Their political ideologies often embrace the rights and voices of the very populations who now stand in opposition to them. Additionally, cancel culture has given rise to one of the most contentious clauses in literary contracts these days: the so-called morals clause, which allows publishers to back out of a book deal if the writer is simply accused of inappropriate behavior or holding offensive ideas. Here are some examples of moral clauses:

In the event that Author is publicly accused of the violation of law, the infringement or invasion of the rights of any third party, inciting infringement or invasion of third-party rights by others, or is otherwise accused of libel, slander, or defamatory conduct, or any other conduct that subjects, or could be reasonably anticipated to subject Author or Publisher to ridicule, contempt, scorn, hatred, or censure by the general public or which is likely to materially diminish the sales of the Work, Publisher may terminate . . .

Publisher may terminate . . . if Author's conduct evidences a lack of due regard for public conventions and morals, or Author commits a crime or any other act that will tend to bring Author into serious contempt, and such behavior would materially damage the Work's reputation or sales.

Publisher may at any time prior to publication choose not to publish the Work if past or future illegal conduct of the Author, inconsistent with the Author's reputation at the time this Agreement is executed and unknown to Publisher, is made public and results in sustained, widespread public condemnation of the Author that materially diminishes the sales potential of the Work. (Authors Guild, 2019)

In other words, some publishing houses are anticipating the possible necessity of canceling their already contracted authors on the basis of their behavior.

Some have argued that cancel culture is about power, aimed at powerful people by groups of people who don't have power and want to express their disapproval in a way that can affect and even perhaps topple the powerful from their position of privilege. Ligaya Mishan (2020) of the *New York Times* affirmed the importance of cancel culture as "a necessary and righteous tool for those with less structural power to wield against those with more power."

Beyond the Literature Classroom: Canceling Out a Culture of Forgiveness

Cancel culture, as we have seen, has chilling effects on literary production and consumption. It also has a significant cost to our culture as a whole. The absolute and sometimes vengeful elements of cancel culture have dangerous implications on social and psychological levels as well. First, there is the issue of a kind of binary judgment by which something is either good or terrible. There is no nuance. President Obama commented on the sometimes brutal lack of ambiguity, especially among young people: "I do get a sense sometimes now among certain young people, and this is accelerated by social media, there is this sense sometimes of: 'The way of me making change is to be as judgmental as possible about other people,'" he said, "and that's enough" (Rueb & Taylor, 2019).

Canceling authors in such an absolute way has led

young people to think they can cancel out each other. It's a different kind of bullying, and bullying may not be an inappropriate descriptor to what has happened to some authors. In some ways, cancel culture is not only affecting young people because of the denial of certain literary experiences; it is creating a particular kind of culture that is regrettable, even dangerous, as it moves beyond the domain of the literary. We are creating a culture that can lead to a kind of heartless bullying. It also prevents the development of what William Perry (1970) categorized as relativistic thought, the ability to inhabit and understand perspectives that are different from one's own, a cognitive stance that is critical for a healthy educational culture as well as a democracy.

Cancel culture is not only intellectually impoverished; it's spiritually impoverished as well. In the fiercely absolute world of cancel culture, there just doesn't seem to be any room for forgiveness, a major cornerstone of all major religions and even our own Constitution. Unlike cancel culture, forgiveness does not seek to destroy; it seeks to repair. The absolute arbiter word of cancel culture means that there can't really be any room for discussion or evaluation. In a *New York Times* article entitled, "Tales from the Teenage Cancel Culture," Sanam Yar and Jonah Engel

Bromwich (2020), quote a 17-year-old who said that people should be held accountable for their actions, whether they're famous or not, but that canceling someone "takes away the option for them to learn from their mistakes and kind of alienates them."

Teaching Literature in the Era of Cancel Culture: Some Alternative Approaches

Teachers of literature face a difficult dilemma when it comes to cancel culture and the literary texts that we teach. Journalist and educator Betty Cotter (2018) expresses it succinctly:

> As more and more male writers stand accused of inappropriate behavior, the teacher in me feels conflicted. Should I keep a storyteller off my syllabus if his behavior is misogynistic or predatory? Is it fair to deprive students of writing that might engage them, because the author is not a good person? (para. 10)

In today's era of cancel culture, we teachers of literature seem obligated to perform a kind of moral calculus, measuring the character or moral standing of the writer against the perceived literary and educational value of the text. There are many factors that might go into this calculation, including whether the author is living or dead, the degree to which the author has acknowledged his or her transgressions, the durability or literary significance of the work, and the reasons why the text is being taught, among other factors. If a teacher chooses not to teach a book, he or she is participating in cancel culture, unwittingly or not.

What are some ways of dealing with this dilemma of adhering to one's own moral and pedagogical principles— which should, of course, be consonant? Perhaps we need to consider the case of each book and each other, giving students a choice. Perhaps we should first discuss it, pose it as a moral dilemma. Right now, there is no chance to explore the ambiguities, no nuance, no discussion. We can choose to cancel out the books, but should we do it wordlessly? Should we even try to let students know what they are missing? Here are some pedagogical alternatives to straight up cancel culture.

Make the absence visible
It may indeed be the case that a teacher will choose to remove a book, which many teachers have done with

Sherman Alexie and Junot Díaz, for example. Too often, the text just disappears from the curriculum without any commentary. The students are none the wiser. Perhaps the teacher could offer the case to the students, discussing the work and then also explaining why they chose not to teach it. The text could be offered as an independent reading choice to students who would be made aware of it. In addition, discussing the removal of the text could provide an opportunity to discuss standards of appropriate behavior as well as issues of sexual harassment and assault and, in some cases, issues of gender equity.

Offer alternative texts

Another approach to canceling out a text entirely might be to bundle it with other texts that are related thematically as a kind of text set. Rather than simply teaching a Sherman Alexie text, be it *The Lone Ranger and Tonto Fistfight in Heaven* or *The Absolutely True Diary of a Part-Time Indian*, students could choose which text to read and have intertextual conversations. Relating to Alexie, a text set could focus on some of the themes I articulated earlier such as cultural homelessness, redemption, identity, vanishing and stolen Native American culture, ethnic heritage, displacement, and stereotyping. Here is an example of such a text set:

**Suggested Text Set for Alternatives
to Reading Sherman Alexie**

St. Lucy's Home for Girls Raised by Wolves by Karen
  Russell

Lakota Woman by Mary Crow Dog

There, There by Tommy Orange

If I Ever Get Out of Here by Eric Gansworth

Rain Is Not My Indian Name by Cynthia Leitich Smith

Open Mic: Riffs on Life Between Cultures in Ten Voices
  edited by Mitali Perkins

Teach texts from a theoretical perspective

Whether to consider the relationship between the author
and his or her work is a notable theoretical issue. A staple of nearly every public school literature textbook is
an obligatory biographical sketch of the author. Those
sketches animate the prevailing sense, regardless of
whether it is fully articulated, that knowing something
about the writer can enhance our understanding of the
work. Betty Cotter (2020) offers the following examples:

> Before they can understand that slim lyric poem
> "The Red Wheelbarrow," they must know that Wil-
> liam Carlos Williams was a doctor on a house call
> in a poor African American neighborhood when he

spotted the titular farm conveyance upon which "so much depends." To appreciate Poe's story "The Cask of Amontillado," it helps to understand the rage the author felt toward a literary rival. (para. 14)

We can all think of other biographical nuggets that we have deemed essential to our students' literary understanding, whether it is Emily Dickenson's isolation, Fitzgerald's lifestyle and troubled marriage to Zelda, Mary Shelly's mother's death at her birth, or Sylvia Plath's relationships with male figures and her eventual suicide. We use these as interpretive touchstones.

I should note, however, that all of these biographical facts are directed back into the work to help us read it, not to make certain that we don't read it. In general, most of biographical discussion has focused on authors who are dead, not contemporary authors.

On the other hand, there has been a strong literary tradition nurtured by the New Criticism, which eschews the use of authors' biographies and other contextual considerations. Advocating for a closed approach to reading literature, the New Critics movement contended that the reading and interpretation of the text should be limited to what is in the text and advocated the use of the application of literary nameable devices, such as rhyme, meter, setting, ambiguity, irony, tension, characterization, and plot.

Because the New Critics movement was also dismissive of the importance or relevance of a reader's response to the work, I always considered this formalist school of literary study to be anathema to the work I hoped to do with adolescent readers. Now, because of the long and destructive shadow of cancel culture, I yearn to separate the author from the work.

In *Beyond the Culture Wars: How Teaching the Conflicts Can Revitalize American Education* (1993), Gerry Graff extended a persuasive invitation to a divided literature professoriate, one that found itself on opposite sides of a culture war not unlike what we are experiencing today. He suggested that we invite our students into to the controversies surrounding the teaching of particular texts by actually teaching the controversy itself. Graff might well suggest that we teach this theoretical controversy as part of literary study. For example, I have sometimes offered students the poem "Mushroom" by Sylvia Plath (Appleman, 2015) without the author's name and sometimes even without the title, drawing different kinds of literary interpretations. Then, after giving them the name of the poem and a brief author bio, we see how the interpretations can change.

The question of the role the author's life should play in literary study is a significant one. Why not present it to our students as a theoretical dilemma, rather than simply withhold a text based on our judgment of the author's life? Recently, a high school in Minneapolis did just that. A team of English teachers introduced students to the controversy surrounding Sherman Alexie, whose book, *The Absolutely True Diary of a Part-Time Indian*, had previously been a staple in the literature curriculum. The students read articles about the accusations of sexual misconduct, including some that strongly advocated his books should be removed from high school classrooms. They also read reviews of his work as well as previews of *The Absolutely True Diary of a Part-Time Indian*. The students spent two days discussing the controversy, and then took a vote, deciding they wanted to read the novel. Alternative choices were offered to any students who wanted to opt out of the reading. There weren't any.

Cancel the cancellation

Another option is to simply ignore the controversies altogether, to not alter the curriculum based on either contemporary incidents with individual authors or revisionist histories as we reappraise the misogyny of authors like Poe, Hemingway, Fitzgerald, and more. We needn't vouch for the authors, one way or another. Perhaps we should simply present their books and have students read them, prepared as we always should be to offer an alternative if it is required.

Conclusion

Cancel culture may indeed have enforced some accountability upon powerful artists who abused their power. It may have turned silent witnesses into emboldened advocates speaking against injustice and reprehensible actions against other human beings. On the other hand, at its worst, cancel culture has repressed both the production and consumption of literary work in often arbitrary and mistaken ways. Its social corollary of canceling out not only artists and celebrities, but also young people, too, has become a brutal variation on bullying. Its lack of nuance and the lack of opportunity for forgiveness or redemption may teach lessons as unfortunate as any of the transgressions of the authors who have been canceled.

Perhaps there is a way that we can retain some of our literary treasures, both classic and contemporary, and still make all of us accountable to some kind of reasonable moral standard. As good as its original intentions might have been, cancel culture will not get us there. Teachers will need to decide for themselves whether to continue to teach Sherman Alexie or Junot Díaz or recommend the Harry Potter series or the adolescent novels of some now-shunned authors. Let's at least have a conversation about it before we reflexively respond in a way that does nothing to promote critical thinking and offers no room for redemption or forgiveness. Do we really want a society like that? Do we really want young people to experience such a diminished education?

CHAPTER 3

Trigger-Happy

> Art occurs at the intersection of experience and
> danger. It can be risky, subversive, and offensive.
> Literature encompasses ideas both repugnant and
> redemptive.
>
> —DEB STONE

Not too long ago, a sincere and enthusiastic undergraduate met with her advisor, an English professor, to declare her English major and to chat about her
concerns regarding the introductory literature class she
would be taking from him that coming semester.

"I am looking forward to taking your class and
embarking on my English major," she said, "But I also
wanted to tell you that I am easily triggered by a variety
of things, and there are certain topics I will have to avoid."

"Of course," said the professor, eager to accommo-
date his new advisee and welcome her into the frankly

shrinking pool of English majors. "We can most likely work things out in advance of our reading and discussion if you tell me what we need to avoid."

"Well, I can't read anything with violence, of course, no death, really, either. Also, explicit sex and any kind of family discord and dysfunction. That's about it."

"Well," the professor said, dismayed. "I am afraid you have eliminated, not only most of the syllabus of our class, but the corpus of literature writ large. Not only would it be inadvisable for you to take this class, I'm not sure you can be an English major with those restrictions."

The undergraduate sullenly left the office as the professor put his head between his hands and sighed heavily.

Last year at my undergraduate college, a professor who included *The Bluest Eye* by Toni Morrison on her syllabus was confronted by a group of her students even before the class began. "We won't read this book under any conditions," they told her in a joint office hour appointment two days before the class was to begin. "It has incest in it, and that is triggering. We don't think you have a right to assign it or make us read it." The professor found herself in a profound pedagogical, even moral, dilemma. On the one hand, she didn't want to harm or revictimize any of her students. On the other hand, she fervently believes that the novel has a critically significant place in our (finally) diversifying literary heritage and in the context of her woman's studies course and deserves to be read. She also believes that creating classes, choosing readings, and preparing to discuss and explore even controversial readings is a central part of her role and responsibilities as a professor. She admits to both some surprise and perhaps even indignation that her future students were both telling her what to teach (or not teach) without affording her an opportunity to create a supportive learning environment in which difficult topics could be discussed. What complicated her decision was that the students (as is frequently the case) were arguing from a place of deeply held principle rather than personal traumatic experience. In other words, none had been victims themselves of incest; they were standing in political solidarity with others, not even specific others in their acquaintance, but hypothetical others. They were claiming trauma by proxy, as it were. Their concerns were legitimate, to be sure, but this kind of indirect advocacy can complicate the decisions a teacher makes about what to teach, or in this case, what not to teach, to her students.

Can literature be read without triggering, or, in fact, is part of the role of literature to trigger—that is, to wake and engage our complex set of emotions and experiences? While it is imperative to consider our students' well-being and to teach sensitively, I worry that these considerations will banish some significant texts into silence. The call for trigger warnings (in the case of teaching literature, pre-reading cautions that literature might trigger complex memories or unhealed wounds from previous trauma) clearly has its merits. After all, we teachers have a commitment to do no harm. Yet it is almost impossible to read literature, that unflinching mirror of the human condition, without touching on the kinds of issues that many students ask to be shielded from: death, violence, heartache, childhood and adolescent trauma, illness, and sexuality.

Every generation of students brings a unique set of characteristics into the classroom. While the individual qualities of readers defy generalization, there are often shifts in cultural norms or expectations that affect learning and specifically the climate of the literature classroom. Over the last decade or so, readers and students have been more willing to advocate for their own personal sense of well being in the classroom. This kind of advocacy has been encouraged by an increased awareness of the importance of paying attention to student mental health and the seemingly increased feelings of fragility and vulnerability among students. This trend has given rise to what has come to be known as trigger warnings.

What Are Trigger Warnings?

Trigger warnings are preemptive alerts given by educators about material that could initiate extreme discomfort for learners. At its simplest, a trigger warning is a statement, written or oral, made prior to sharing any content that is potentially disturbing. That content could be written language, a photograph, a video clip, a film or portions of a film, or even content in a lecture. It has become common classroom practice for teachers to warn students that something in that day's lesson or in class material might trigger anxiety, discomfort, outward displays of emotion, or even PTSD. Initially occasional and wholly voluntary, the inclusion of trigger warnings has become pro forma, even mandatory in some academic settings, especially as part of a syllabus to provide a kind of blanket, preemptive warning.

According to the University of Michigan, here are some topics that might require trigger warnings:

- sexual assault
- abuse
- child abuse/pedophilia/incest
- animal cruelty or animal death

- self-harm and suicide
- eating disorders, body hatred, and fat phobia
- violence
- pornographic content
- kidnapping and abduction
- death or dying
- pregnancy/childbirth
- miscarriages/abortion
- blood
- mental illness and ableism
- racism and racial slurs
- sexism and misogyny
- classism
- hateful language directed at religious groups (e.g., Islamophobia, anti-Semitism)
- transphobia and trans misogyny
- homophobia and heterosexism

(University of Michigan, 2021)

The list is not only dauntingly exhaustive; it includes many topics that would be nearly impossible to completely avoid within the normal course of reading both classic and contemporary literature. It would most likely be possible to avoid some of these topics some of the time, and perhaps even some of these topics all of the time, but it would probably be impossible to avoid all of these topics all of the time in the practice of reading literature.

Where Did Trigger Warnings Come From?

The idea of trigger warnings first appeared in the late 1990s. According to writer and researcher Deb Stone (2014),

> The term seems to have originated from the use of the word "trigger" to indicate something that cues a physiological response, the way pollen may trigger an allergy attack. A trigger in a firearm is a lever that activates the sequence of firing a gun, so it is not surprising that the word was commandeered by those working in the field of psychology to indicate objects and sensations that cause neurological firing in the brain, which in turn cause feelings and thoughts to occur. (para. 6)

Since the initial appearance of trigger warnings in the psychiatric literature and then in nonacademic settings, such as media from websites to mainstream publications, their use has become increasingly common in both secondary and postsecondary classrooms. In fact, at some colleges and universities it has become an expected, if not required, practice (American Association of University Professors, 2014). Many teachers view trigger warnings as a part of their required practice, and students of nearly all grade levels have come to both expect and require them.

Why Trigger Warnings Can Be Useful

As we have learned more about trauma and post-traumatic disorders, educators have realized that there are triggering events that can affect the well-being of students, even students who seem to present themselves as well-adjusted young people. There may be certain specific material that might cause a student to reflexively respond because the material bears some relationship to a previous trauma. While learning can and perhaps even should be uncomfortable, no one really learns when they are in emotional distress. A response to an unexpected stimulus can prevent a student from being able to focus or even to think, let alone learn new material. In some cases, an extreme response may necessitate that a student leaves the classroom. Here is an excellent explanation from the University of Waterloo Centre for Teaching Excellence (n.d.):

Proponents of trigger warnings contend that certain course content can impact the well-being and academic performance of students who have experienced corresponding traumas in their own lives. Such students might not yet be ready to confront a personal trauma in an academic context. Other students might indeed be ready to confront a personal trauma in an academic context but will benefit from a forewarning of certain topics so that they can brace themselves prior to (for example) participating in a classroom discussion about it. Considered from this perspective, trigger warnings give students increased autonomy over their learning, and are an affirmation that the instructor cares about their well-being. (para. 2)

In other words, trigger warnings can be a necessary part of a teacher's toolkit, residing with other strategies and methodologies to ensure student learning. In some cases, offering a trigger warning may make the teaching or at least the receiving of certain materials possible. It is one thing to offer material that might make certain students uncomfortable for both emotional and intellectual reasons; it's quite another to try to offer material and engage student learning if a student becomes upset. If students are emotionally hijacked by some content, they won't be able to focus on it. As Julie Winterich (2015) explains,

> The intent of a trigger warning is to acknowledge that some students may need to prepare themselves before engaging with explicit texts or films that might otherwise catch them off guard. But what preparing oneself looks like differs based on where each specific student is in the healing process. (para. 10)

In some ways, offering a trigger or, in other words, preparing students to receive what might feel like unreceivable material could actually help them learn it. One middle school social studies teacher, for example, believes that he has an imperative to teach his students about the brutal reality of slavery, since it is such an important and shameful part of American history. To not teach it would be inexcusable. On the other hand, he has begun to question his ability to continue to teach about slavery because there have been numerous incidents of parents and students of color reporting that learning about slavery in a classroom setting, whether it be in a history classroom or a literature classroom, is too traumatizing. There have been similar incidents with teaching about the Holocaust as well. Of course, learning about these historical atrocities is painful. But what are the consequences of having students not learn about them? (Khalid & Snyder, 2021).

In order to be able to prepare students to learn difficult material, some teachers have offered a trigger warning such as this one:

> Our classroom provides an open space for the critical and civil exchange of ideas. Some readings and other content in this course will include topics that some students may find offensive and/or traumatizing. I'll aim to forewarn students about potentially disturbing content and I ask all students to help to create an atmosphere of mutual respect and sensitivity. (University of Waterloo, n.d.)

Or this one:

> This course may include readings, media, and discussion around topics such as sexual assault, domestic violence, stalking, physical violence, and identity-based discrimination and harassment. I acknowledge that this content may be difficult. I also encourage you to care for your safety and well-being. (University Health Service, UW Madison, n.d.)

According to the teachers who use them, trigger warnings like this allow them to continue to teach the possibly triggering material and still have a sense that they are taking some protective measures for the well-being of their students. It is both a protection for the students as well as protection for the teachers, since teachers have increasingly been made responsible for providing some kind of warning to students. To not do so seems to violate what from the students' perspective is some kind of social contract and what from an administrative or institutional perspective is some kind of professional obligation.

The Problem With Trigger Warnings

However, despite the common-sense appeal to educators for the well-being of individual students, trigger warnings have plenty of detractors as well. Several scholars have made the case that trigger warnings constitute an infringement on academic freedom (American Association of University Professors, 2014). Some detractors believe it is impossible to predict what material might be triggering for students. Others believe that a simple verbal warning could not stave off a true post-traumatic effect, an objection validated by mental health professionals

(Jarrett, 2019). In fact, according to the American Psychological Association (2017), "There is little support for the idea that offering generic classroom warnings about sensitive topics is beneficial to students in general."

Still others assert that a forewarning might take the power out of material whose value is precisely because of its emotional impact. In other words, trigger warnings might act as spoilers for the emotional impact a novel, film, or other material is supposed to have. Surprise, discomfort, sadness, even repulsion, are sometimes necessary ingredients for creating the kind of emotional dissonance that may be required for the full impact and intent of certain texts. Some observers worry that trigger warnings can stifle candid, unfettered discussion about the very kinds of important issues best explored in a nurturing learning environment. They worry that trigger warnings as well as the avoidance of difficult subjects would make it less likely that important topics would be explored precisely in the kind of supportive and carefully constructed educational environment that would make such conversations both possible and productive. Others claim, perhaps cavalierly, that life doesn't come with trigger warnings and that it's not fair to expect schools to equip students with an unrealistic expectation that they will be both warned and protected from the unexpected challenges and unpleasantness all of us inevitably face. The University of Waterloo (n.d.) offers this pragmatic perspective:

> Some fear that trigger warnings unnecessarily insulate students from the often-harsh realities of the world with which academics need to engage. Others are concerned that trigger warnings establish a precedent of making instructors or universities legally responsible for protecting students from emotional trauma. Still others argue that it is impossible to anticipate all the topics that might be potentially triggering for students.

Trigger warnings have also come under increased scrutiny about their relative ineffectiveness in preventing students from experiencing trauma in the classroom. In an experimental study (Jones et al., 2020), a team of scientists found that trigger warning are generally not effective and concluded the following:

> The research suggests that trigger warnings are unhelpful for trauma survivors, college students, trauma-naïve individuals, and mixed groups of participants. Given this consistent conclusion, we find no

evidence-based reason for educators, administrators, or clinicians to use trigger warnings. (p. 915)

The AAUP (2014) voices concern that requiring the presence of trigger warnings threatens the academic freedom of teachers. It also asserts the following:

The classroom is not the appropriate venue to treat PTSD, which is a medical condition that requires serious medical treatment. Trigger warnings are an inadequate and diversionary response. Medical research suggests that triggers for individuals can be unpredictable, dependent on networks of association. So color, taste, smell, and sound may lead to flashbacks and panic attacks as often as the mention of actual forms of violence such as rape and war. The range of any student's sensitivity is thus impossible to anticipate. (p. 3)

Trigger Warnings Can Ruin the Literary Experience

In addition to uncertainty about the relative usefulness of trigger warnings, there are ways in which the harm they may cause seems more definitive than the help they might offer. This is especially true in the potential effects of trigger warnings on response to literature. Trigger warnings in the literature classroom can have negative consequences for both students and teachers. While it can limit the possibilities of students' authentic responses to literature, it can also complicate the teaching of literature. Examples abound of the chilling effects of trigger warnings on literature instruction. Teachers at both the secondary and college levels are reconsidering the place of Shakespeare in the literature curriculum as they juggle complaints about violence and sex, with some proudly refusing to teach it at all. In fact, in a recent *Education Week* article, middle school teacher Christina Torres (2019) wondered "if Shakespeare is actually good for my students to read," and said "When I read *Romeo and Juliet* with my students, I pause, give a thumbs-down, and say 'Boo' when the play says something misogynistic." As Winterich (2015) notes, even William Butler Yeats's "Leda and the Swan" or Ovid's *Metamorphosis* might require a trigger warning these days, since a rape is involved in both. *The Great Gatsby* has also been deemed to require prereading trigger warnings because of a "variety of scenes that reference gory, abusive and misogynistic violence" (Jarrett, 2019).

If there is a suicide, for example, in a novel or a death of a major character, teachers are advised to warn students ahead of time, sometimes removing all of the potential power of the piece of literature. Because of the potentially dampening or spoiling effects of trigger warnings on literature, some teachers have found that perhaps the easiest thing to do is to not teach the piece at all. At Oberlin, for example, Chinua Achebe's *Things Fall Apart* has come under scrutiny because its content includes racism, colonialism, religious persecution, violence, and suicide. As Jill Filipovic (2014) points out, trigger warnings, in addition to serving as "literary spoilers," also "set the tone for reading and understanding the book. It skews students' perceptions. It highlights particular issues as necessarily more upsetting than others, and directs students to focus on particular themes that have been singled out by the professor as traumatic." Somewhat ironically, calling attention to specific instances of a text through trigger warnings can result in the instances being highlighted, sensationalized, and overemphasized.

The Value of Witnessing

Recently, I was trying to decide whether to assign a documentary about "Strange Fruit," the evocative song by Billie Holiday that offers a metaphorical treatment of lynching with black bodies hanging in poplar trees like "strange fruit." I asked myself whether the documentary was too unsettling to show, even though there were really only a couple of fleeting images that were explicit. I wondered if I should use it and, if I did, what kind of trigger warning would be sufficient and appropriate to let students experience the dramatic intent and brutal subject of the song without being traumatized by it. Just as I was leaning toward not showing the documentary at all, I remembered a segment of the documentary itself, where they showed hundreds of African Americans lined up to see an exhibit on lynching that contained many explicit and disturbing images. Why did those African Americans subject themselves to something so disturbing? Perhaps they felt that in order to understand and if necessary, change something, it had to be confronted.

In notes to an exhibit called "The Legacy of Lynching: Confronting Racial Terror in America," the Brooklyn Museum wrote the following: "Throughout the Brooklyn Museum's history, our exhibitions and public programs have confronted difficult and urgent issues because we believe that great art and courageous conversations contribute to a more just, civic, and empathetic world" (2017).

An important part of the education we strive to provide can, for lack of a better word, be called witnessing. I sometimes have felt like saying to students, "Some people actually suffered this and lived through it; the least you can do is be a witness to it for them." Trigger warnings often keep people away from witnessing something they need to be aware of. In other words, trigger warnings often do more than simply warn people what will happen when they view something. They may discourage people from experiencing something altogether. Deb Stone (2014) eloquently makes the case for witnessing: "We are changed by what we witness. Knowledge helps us prioritize our responsibilities in the world. Don't we want engaged, knowledgeable citizens striving for a better world?" This argument obtains or has relevance for one of the primary functions that literature can serve. As Nadine Gordimer (2001) observed, "Non-fiction uses fact to help us see the lies. Fiction uses metaphor to help us see the truth."

Experiencing Different Points of View

One fundamental premise of education, especially liberal arts education, has been the importance of understanding the perspective and point of view of others. The ability to understand concepts from different perspectives as well as the ability to inhabit, or at least understand, different point of views is generally a hallmark of intellectual maturity and cognitive development. From a developmental perspective, at least according to the cognitive theory of intellectual development posited by William Perry (1970), the task of educators is to help move their students from a dualistic way of thinking to a more complex, relativistic scheme, and finally, to multiplicity. How do we move learners from a dualistic perspective to a relativistic one? By introducing them to other perspectives and ideas that do not necessarily comport with their own. In fact, disagreement, discomfort, and dissonance can be viewed as required for intellectual growth. As Jill Filipovic (2014) writes,

> Students should be pushed to examine their own ideals and be challenged by them. The point of literature and of education is not to promise to meet people where there are but to have the potential to take them somewhere else. It is, hopefully, a space where the student is challenged and sometimes frustrated and sometimes deeply upset, a place where the student's world expands and pushes them to reach the outer edges—not a place that contracts to meet the student exactly where they are. (para. 12)

Importantly, reading literature can offer those different points of view and foster students' intellectual development. In fact, Theory of Mind, the idea that human beings have the capacity to recognize and understand that other people have thoughts and desires that are different from one's own, has been shown to be enhanced by the reading of fiction:

> The currently predominant view is that literary fiction—often described as narratives that focus on in-depth portrayals of subjects' inner feelings and thoughts—can be linked to theory of mind processes, especially those that are involved in the understanding or simulation of the affective characteristics of the subjects. (Kidd & Castano, 2013, p. 377)

Who Is Protecting Whom?

Trigger warnings can be seen to be both patronizing and infantilizing, especially to those they are ostensibly designed to protect. There is a potential backlash against protecting particular groups who may seem to be marginalized. A directive to issue a trigger warning on behalf of someone else can be perceived as overprotective or even presumptuous. Further, it can stigmatize or essentialize a particular group by signifying its members as powerless and vulnerable. Trigger warnings are largely perceived as protecting young women and, to a lesser extent, other marginalized groups. That the warnings hinge on topics that are more likely to affect the lives of marginalized groups contributes to the general perception of members of those groups as weak, vulnerable, and other.

Teaching Literature in the Era of Trigger Warnings

Trigger warnings have been the source of a great deal of ambivalence among educators for many of the reasons we have discussed in this chapter. Teachers want their classrooms to be safe and productive spaces and do not want students to be traumatized or rendered into a state in which they feel emotionally incapable of learning. Most teachers also recognize the increased vulnerability and fragility of many of our students as well as our increased collective awareness and understanding of trauma and post-traumatic stress.

It seems impossible to predict all of the potential

triggers for students, and some educators would assert that it isn't their job to anticipate what might be psychologically triggering to their students. As we have discussed, there are also issues of academic freedom as well. According to the American Association of University Professors (2014), institutional requirements or even suggestions that faculty use trigger warnings interfere with faculty academic freedom in the choice of course materials and teaching methods. Faculty might feel pressured into notifying students about course content for fear that some students might find it disturbing. Of course, there may be instances when a teacher judges it necessary to alert students to potentially difficult material and that is his or her right. Administrative requirements are different from individual faculty decisions. Administration regulation constitutes interference with academic freedom; faculty judgment is a legitimate exercise of autonomy.

Somehow, then, we need to strike a balance between pedagogical overprotection and negligence. We need to strike a balance between accusations of coddling the American mind and of the need to heed the sensibilities of today's hyperaware and perhaps hypersensitive students.

Some Alternative Approaches

What are some substitutes for trigger warnings in the classroom? What follows are some possible alternative approaches to the sometimes problematic use of trigger warnings in the literature classroom.

Offer alternative texts

The era of one text for an entire class is long over. Given the diversity of contemporary classrooms, the variability of students' reading experiences, and the differences in students reading abilities, many teachers in both secondary and postsecondary classes offer students a choice of texts that may be thematically related but different in their treatment of triggerable material. Similar to the strategy discussed with regard to cancel culture, this strategy allows students to make choices and doesn't involuntarily impose a potentially objectionable text on all students. It also preserves the text as a possibility for some students to read.

Give an overview at the beginning of the class

Somewhat related to a trigger warning, but more integrated and less specifically reactive, teachers might offer a kind of meta warning as a way of introducing the nature of the content of the class. Positioning the warning this way has a couple of advantages over offering periodic warnings to individual texts. First, it provides an overview into the content of the course. Here is an example of this kind of overarching trigger.

> At times during this course, we will be discussing topics that may be disturbing, even traumatizing, to some students. If you are aware of particular course material that may be traumatizing to you, I'd be happy to discuss any concerns you may have with it before it comes up in class. Similarly, if you ever wish to discuss your personal reactions to such material with the class or with me afterwards, I welcome such discussion as an appropriate part of our coursework. If you ever feel the need to step outside during one of these discussions, either for a short time or for the rest of the class session, you may always do so without academic penalty. You will, however, be responsible for any material you miss. If you do leave the room for a significant time, please make arrangements to get notes from another student or see me individually to discuss the situation. (Bristow et al., 2015, para. 59)

Give students agency by
teaching the controversy

In *Beyond the Culture Wars* (1993), Gerry Graff forwards the idea of teaching the conflict:

> I argue that the best solution to today's conflicts over culture is to teach the conflicts themselves, making them part of our object of study. (p. 12)

So, rather than preemptively decide that a particular text is too touchy, too volatile, too sensitive, too triggering, why not let students weigh in on whether the text is teachable and perhaps even more importantly what might be the value of being in contact with potentially painful and disturbing material.

These kinds of discussions can be particularly valuable in helping students weigh the relative merits of different perspectives, develop their own positions, hone their aesthetic sensibilities, and learn to craft reasoned and reasonable arguments. What is happening currently in the educational landscape is precisely what Graff lamented three decades ago—students are not "playing a more active role" in the controversies, because we, the teachers, have already made curricular decisions that will shut down debate (1993, p. 11).

Have a discussion about triggers and their pros and cons

There is considerable and interesting literature, both pedagogical and psychological, about the use of trigger warnings in academic settings. There are strong arguments for their advisability and well as increasing pressure from both students and institutions to offer trigger warnings on a regular basis. On the other hand, as has been discussed above, there is little evidence that trigger warnings actually protect students from further trauma, especially students who are suffering from PTSD. Discussing the advantages and disadvantages of trigger warnings with students might be preferable to determining a priori whether a trigger warning should be provided for any particular text.

Work with students individually

Sometimes we make large group corrections when the issue may deeply impact only a handful of students. While the potential damage is no less important because it affects only a couple of individuals, it might be possible to let individual students opt out of a certain portion of a class because it might be triggering. For example, I remember as a high school teacher preemptively excusing a student who had recently been in a car accident before we read

Karl Shapiro's graphic poetic treatment of a car accident, "Auto Wreck." Another student, who had recently buried his mother, elected not to read Edgar Allen Poe's "The Cask of Amontillado." In other words, some texts are triggering to individuals because of specific traumas they may have had, but those individual incidents may not be sufficient cause to provide trigger warnings for the entire class or to refrain from teaching that particular literary text.

Use reason and moderation in choosing criteria

Recent use of trigger warnings seems to be sometimes extreme and reactionary, although there may be some images, concepts, events, or topics that can generally be agreed upon as unsuitable for classroom consumption. Establishing a community standard after discussion might be one way of approaching this as an alternative to offering perhaps unnecessary protection for vaguely disturbing or potentially disturbing material. The Centre for Teaching Excellence at the University of Waterloo (n.d.) offers the following advice:

- Give your students as much advance notice as possible about potentially disturbing content. A day's notice might not be enough for a student to prepare emotionally, but two weeks might be.

- Try to "scaffold" a disturbing topic to students. For example, when beginning a history unit on the Holocaust, don't start with graphic photographs from Auschwitz. Instead, begin by explaining the historical context, then verbally describe the conditions within the concentration camps, and then introduce the photographic record as needed. Whenever possible, allow students to progress through upsetting material at their own pace.
- Allow students to interact with disturbing material outside of class. A student might feel more vulnerable watching a documentary about sexual assault while in a classroom than in the security of his or her home.
- Provide captions when using video materials: some content is easier to watch while reading captions than while listening to the audio.
- When necessary, provide written descriptions of graphic images as a substitute for the actual visual content.
- When disturbing content is under discussion, check in with your students from time to time: ask them how they are doing, whether they need a break, and so on. Let them know that you are aware that the material in question is emotionally challenging.

- Advise students to be sensitive to their classmates' vulnerabilities when they are preparing class presentations.
- Help your students understand the difference between emotional trauma and intellectual discomfort: the former is harmful, as is triggering it in the wrong context (such as in a classroom rather than in therapy); the latter is fundamental to a university education—it means our ideas are being challenged as we struggle to resolve cognitive dissonance.

Conclusion

Like many pedagogical practices gone awry, trigger warnings have a benevolent and well-intentioned origin—to protect students from harm. Teachers are motivated to create safe space in which their students can learn and of course have no interest in retraumatizing traumatized students. However, in practice, trigger warnings have had a chilling effect on the teaching and learning of literature. Based on dubious psychological evidence, the power of literature is often sacrificed to protect anticipated, often debilitating discomfort. Yet, it also can serve to protect students from encountering difficult ideas and witnessing particular kinds of topics that might be important to their intellectual development. Pressure to offer trigger warnings comes from several directions. Institutions are in danger of trampling on the academic freedom of teachers who do take seriously the charge to create safe but challenging environments for all of their students. Students, too, may sometimes be engaging in self-censoring behavior that is at its worst indulgent and stultifying, closing off important avenues of content.

While there surely may be a case in some classes for some content to be introduced with trigger warnings, my argument here is that they are both misused and overused, to the detriment of literary education, often without any real benefit to the students. Let us reconsider the concept and the use of trigger warnings, and reaffirm the notion that true education is never safe and that our obligation to protect students does not outweigh our obligation to challenge them and offer them the opportunity to witness all that is a part of the human condition.

CHAPTER 4

Wakening to Woke

No book is genuinely free from political bias. The opinion that art should have nothing to do with politics is itself a political attitude.

GEORGE ORWELL

In this cultural moment, there is a tsunami of protest about scores of literary texts, woke waves that are drowning the reputations of authors and submerging texts, from classics to not-even-yet-published young adult novels. Even Dr. Seuss, venerable author of children's books, has been caught up in the fray. Yes, that's right: As of March 2021, six of the beloved author's books will no longer be published, due to images that have been determined by the Seuss estate to be both racist and stereotypical. Reactions to this publishing decision are divided along predictable ideological lines, with conservatives decrying it as another example of cancel culture while social justice educators applaud the move as an example of increased sensitivity to representations of diverse populations and an acknowledgement of the important role literature plays in shaping the worldview of children. These two sides of the debate seem rigid in their positions, yet there is a middle ground that this latest incident begs to call out. On the one hand, there is good reason to raise questions about representation in everything our students read. What we offer students to experience in and out of the classroom shapes not only their ideas about the world around them but their ideas about themselves as well. On the other hand, there seems to be an extreme, almost reactionary response, lacking in nuance and thoughtfulness, to overcorrect, to paint with a broad brush and eliminate any material that is possibly offensive in any way to anyone. Thus, some valued cultural texts are summarily abandoned. Perhaps even more importantly, we collectively forsake an opportunity to discuss the issues that undergird this and other recent controversies: issues such as representation, authenticity, marginalization, essentialism, sexism, homophobia, and racism, to name a just a few.

Let me be clear. Significant curriculum change is vital to ensure that our students' literary education is relevant for everyone. Both the stories and the storytellers need to fully reflect and narrate the diversity of experiences and perspectives of our students. It is absolutely shameful that the ten most commonly taught novels in high school literature curriculum have barely changed in the last 50 years. In addition to centering more diverse voices in the literature curriculum, a critical goal in itself, educators need to become increasingly aware of the kinds of damaging portrayals that are regularly found in the literature we assign— portrayals that belittle, marginalize, and demean others. Clearly, there are some texts that don't deserve to be taught, some material that needs to be reconsidered and then perhaps permanently removed from the academic fare we serve our children. There are some perspectives and positions that need to be challenged, interrogated, even repudiated, while there are other previously excluded and silenced perspectives that need to be introduced and integrated into our curricula.

Other chapters in this book focus on how individual authors are canceled because of their personal behavior or positions, or on how specific subject matter and topics are burdened by mandatory trigger warnings. This chapter focuses on the casualties of our most recent culture war, the texts themselves: texts that have become increasingly problematic in these troublesome and divisive times in which we find ourselves. These issues render myriad works too troublesome to teach. Many texts have been sent to the pedagogical trash heap because they have been deemed culturally insensitive. Sometimes the charge of insensitivity springs from the use of offensive and unacceptable language, such as what is commonly termed "the n-word." In other cases, the charge of cultural insensitivity is leveled because character portrayals veer into the stereotypical. Other objections, grounded in issues of authenticity, accuse some authors of a kind of literary cultural appropriation, as in the recent flap over *American Dirt*, as we discussed in Chapter 2, when a white author narrates a harrowing tale of Mexican refugees. This raises the thorny question of who is entitled to tell which stories, a consideration that can redraw the boundaries of authorial license.

This chapter examines these different challenges and attempts to establish some guidelines to help teachers of literature determine when texts may be too insensitive, inappropriate, or damaging to read and when they may have been unfairly censored or banished. The purpose of this chapter is to identify the multiple ways in which some texts have become so troublesome that they are rendered unteachable. By thinking through the myriad ways that texts are troubled and challenged, we can then consider how to avoid blanket banishment and still face the undergirding issues that legitimately call these texts into question. Perhaps the question is not whether they should be taught, but how they should be taught.

In decades past, the banning and even in some cases the burning of books was most frequently the province of cultural conservatives who were afraid that certain material would corrupt or damage young readers in a variety of ways. Some books, such as *1984* and, ironically, the book-burning-focused *Fahrenheit 451* were banned because of their political ideology; others were banned because they were deemed to be vulgar or too sexually explicit. More recently, books have been banned because they portray controversial topics in positive lights, such as same-sex relationships and explicit sexual encounters of any kind. Still others are banned because they are perceived to be harmful to impressionable and vulnerable readers because they include topics such as bullying, adolescent suicide, substance abuse, and other forms of self-harm.

Now, however, the ideological impetus for the censoring and even banning of books seems to have moved from the conservative right to the progressive left. A combination of social justice warriors and righteous guardians of what has been unfortunately termed "politically correct" have appointed themselves to monitor and correct what gets read and what gets taught, both in and out of school. These arbiters seek to determine the teachability of certain texts. In some cases, their collective objections have actually prevented or interrupted the publication of certain texts, including unpublished YA novels or children's classics, such as the aforementioned Dr. Seuss books. Today we find ourselves in the middle of a culture war that has bitterly divided former intellectual and pedagogical allies and brought together unlikely alliances from the left and from the right. The casualties in this war include not only the books themselves but the opportunity, even the necessity, to confront the uncomfortable: to learn from history, to understand the dynamics of changing culture, and to see what both evolution and revolution bring to our cultural awaking and mutual coexistence.

The Cult of Presentism

Although most critics of troublesome texts are generally well-motivated in their concern for inclusion and equity, there are several significant shortcomings to their articulated objections to the texts they target. For the most part, many of these objections lack any attempt to contextualize the books historically; hence, they are read and ultimately judged ahistorically. Too many cultural commentators superimpose contemporary sensibilities onto texts that reflect realities and cultural norms very different from the present. What is particularly troubling about this current spate of objections to various texts is what Jeff Snyder and Amna Khalid (2021) call the "tyranny of presentism." There are several issues with this kind of reflexive insistence on reading texts through the lens of contemporary culture. First, if an author portrays a cultural reality that excludes current considerations of diversity that we currently and rightfully insist upon, it may very well be because that reality is an accurate depiction of the times in which they lived. For example, even Shakespeare's reviled treatment of Shylock as an anti-Semitic portrayal of a moneylender can be viewed differently from a historical lens that considers the kinds of occupations that were available to Jews during Shakespeare's time. In other words, Shylock as a moneylender is not simply a unidimensional anti-Semitic trope; it has a basis in historical fact. As another example, although the role of women in society has changed markedly over the last few centuries, some authors have been censored for a portrayal of women that accurately reflects the sexist mores, unequal treatment, gender discrimination, and limited opportunities for women of prior, less enlightened times. This includes Hemingway's *For Whom the*

Bell Tolls, Fitzgerald's *The Great Gatsby*, and even Mark Twain's *Adventures of Huckleberry Finn*, which is usually criticized for its portrayals of characters of color, as well as issues with language, but has problematic portrayals of female characters as well.

We can rightfully critique those times and their often misogynistic worldviews, but the texts provide an accurate if politically incorrect window into the flawed and unenlightened past. If literature is indeed a reflection of the worldview and life of the author as he or she lived it, doesn't it seem imperative that we should study the texts from a historical perspective? Is it reasonable to hold texts written decades, even centuries ago, to 21st-century sensibilities and standards? We can discuss what is wrong with how a particular society is portrayed, what aspects of an author's ideology are revealed in the portrayal, and whether they trouble or interrogate certain elements of that society or reflect them unthinkingly. We can even discuss how important it was for that society to change and move beyond its strictures. That kind of reading, however, is different from dismissing something historical as inappropriate to study because it doesn't reflect 21st-century standards. This is a kind of retrospective accounting and accountability that is neither fair nor fitting.

It is unsettling to consider what students are learning when they are encouraged to judge characters from a 21st-century set of standards that doesn't map onto the historical context in which the text was produced. This kind of reading is actually a misreading. As Alan Jacobs notes in *Breaking Bread with the Dead* (2020), "The reader who instantly translates the subject or story of a book into present-day terms often is not having a genuine encounter with the book at all." Jacobs quotes Milan Kundera's *The Book of Laughter and Forgetting* (1980):

> ['T']he first step in liquidating a people . . . is to erase its memory. Destroy its books, its culture, its history then have somebody write new books, manufacture a new culture, invent a new history. Before long, a nation will begin to forget what it is and what it was. (part 1, section 2)

This is a powerful reminder of how important it is to teach who we have been as well as who we are striving to become. For example, in order to achieve a racially just society, we have to reckon with the legacy of slavery. Yet increasingly, both social studies and literature teachers have been cautioned against teaching books that focus on that topic because it is triggering. Not only is it inaccurate, even a misreading, to read or to teach texts without attention to their historical context, it is also dangerous to obliterate all traces of a past that we need to come to terms with in order to make certain that we don't repeat it. Jacobs (2020) admits,

> I am aware that I have taken on a difficult task here: attention to the past is a hard sell. I want to argue that you can't understand the place and the time you're in by immersion; the opposite's true. You have to step out and away and back and forward, and you have to do it regularly. Then you come back to the here and now and say: Ah. That's how it is. (p. 23)

In *The Company We Keep* (1988), Wayne Booth discusses this kind of "doctrinal criticism," and reminds us to consider the difference between art and proselytizing. Booth discusses the responsibility of both the writer and the reader in this regard and argues for a way to consider both the ethics and literary form of a particular piece of literature in a deliberate manner, a manner that doesn't conflate our reservations about—for lack of a better word—the doctrine or politics of the piece with aesthetic considerations of its form. This kind of dual consideration seems to have been lost in the most recent challenges to texts. Once a text is labeled offensive or inappropriate because of its content, its aesthetic properties are rendered either irrelevant or not sufficiently strong to counteract the offensive attributes.

As a collective of educators and scholars, we have thankfully grown in our awareness of the degree to which certain groups of people have been marginalized, shortchanged, and mistreated. Rather than eliminate texts whose antiquated and unenlightened worldviews offend us, perhaps their problematic point of view is a reason to continue to read and reflect on them, not a reason not to. As *Chicago Tribune* writer Heidi Stevens (2021) notes,

> Rounding up and eliminating the remnants of all that harm isn't always the answer. A college professor showed us D. W. Griffith's 1915 "Birth of a Nation" during a lesson on racist propaganda, and viewing it likely provided a more powerful lesson than reading about it. The Chicago Monuments Project may decide to add plaques or parallel installations for many of the pieces they're examining. (para. 16)

It might provide a more powerful lesson to learn about the harmful beliefs that undergird and are perpetuated by a particular piece of art—by watching, reading, and analyzing it—rather than by eliminating it completely.

The Complicated Case of #DisruptTexts

This notion of reading the text and dealing with its underlying -isms—misogyny, racism, homophobia, anti-Semitism, and so on— is one of the guiding impulses behind #DisruptTexts, one of the most popular movements for the reconsideration of the secondary school literary canon. According to their website, #DisruptTexts is a "crowdsourced, grassroots effort by teachers for teachers to challenge the traditional canon in order to create a more inclusive, representative, and equitable language arts curriculum."

There are many things to admire about this particular movement. First, there is concerted effort to help curate a more equitable and inclusive curriculum, to center diverse voices. Many exciting texts and authors have been added to the secondary literature curriculum because of the activism of groups like this one. In fact, #Disrupt-Texts has created some thoughtful and engaging curriculum guides for new and diverse texts that are marketed by Penguin to help bring equity to the classroom or library (Penguin Classroom, n.d.). The intent of these guides is to help diversify the literature curriculum, to offer more texts by authors of color featuring characters of color, to help young readers of color find reading material that reflects their reality, and to encourage teachers to assess the biases inherent in their traditional curricula. It also encourages teachers to check their own biases—about literature, about the canon, and about what they teach to whom. It suggests pairing texts, an interesting and profitable way to put texts in conversation with one another, to consider how one text fills the gaps of another. It asks students to read both texts and worlds through a critical literacy lens, to lay bare the biases and assumptions that undergird the text and its author. In some ways, we are advocating for a similar approach: Don't simply ban the texts, but rather disrupt or reread them. Their goal is often unfairly misinterpreted as advocating for the banishing of texts.

Despite the positive intentions and material changes in curriculum associated with this approach, there are some issues with this initiative, issues that characterize some of the most significant problems of the movement to eliminate certain texts from the secondary high school curriculum. In raising these issues, I want to acknowledge and repudiate some of the unfair vitriol that the #DisruptTexts movement has received from news outlets such as the *Washington Post* and from individuals. These issues elicit very strong reactions from people on both sides of the issue, whether they are arguing that texts should be preserved or challenged. It might behoove us to consider what is so visceral about reactions to these texts, on both sides.

What is potentially concerning with the approach of #DisruptTexts? After all, it does provide a way to keep texts in the curriculum that are problematic, by troubling or disrupting them. However, the suggested teaching methods judge the appropriateness of the texts, regardless of the era in which they were written, to current modern-day sensibilities, thus turning each text from a complex, and yes, sometimes problematic literary artifact into a one-dimensional, highly flawed springboard. The texts are often flattened, with singular attention to the identity traits of both characters and authors, without any concomitant attention to other dimensions of the text, including literary value, aesthetic qualities, and historical and social relevance. Complex works such as Shakespeare plays can be reduced to cartoonish dimensions by #DisruptTexts, with teaching and learning focused primarily on the negative aspects of the text. Here, for example, is a portion of their position statement on teaching Shakespeare:

- We believe he was a man of his time and that his plays harbor problematic depictions and characterizations.

- We believe that if you must teach him due to school policies and lack of autonomy, or choose to do so autonomously, the only responsible way to do so is by disrupting his plays. We offer our guided discussion questions as a way to begin thinking about how to #DisruptTexts.

The aim, then, seems to be to encourage teachers not to teach Shakespeare unless they are forced to do so. Additionally, any interpretive and aesthetic conclusion about Shakespeare's work and its value has already been reached, not with the students but by the teacher. This is the kind of intellectual and curricular monologue that Graff (1993) opposes. Instead, he encourages teachers to offer students the opportunity to experience opposing viewpoints about a text as well as texts that exist in opposition to each other: "Acknowledging that culture is a debate rather than a monologue does not prevent us from energetically fighting for the truth of our own convictions" (p. 15).

Underestimating Readers

Emily Dickinson once wrote that "There is no frigate like a book." Others have written eloquently about the ways in which literature functions as not only a mirror of our own identity and lived experiences, but also as a window to other people's realities (Sims Bishop, 1990). To make narrow assumptions about what would interest our students based on their own identities underestimates their intellectual capacities as well as their literary imaginations. Many have testified to the power of literature to move us out of ourselves, from Ralph Ellison to James Baldwin (1963), who said, "You read something which you thought only happened to you, and you discover that it happened 100 years ago to Dostoyevsky. This is a very great liberation for the suffering, struggling person, who always thinks that he is alone. This is why art is important."

Those who have worked with the incarcerated have commented eloquently on the degree to which they respond enthusiastically to Shakespeare, one of the hardest hit authors in the #DisruptTexts paradigm. As Khalid and Snyder (2021) point out, "By predetermining which texts will speak to whom based on crude racial and cultural categories, we potentially deprive people of some of the most transformative reading experiences they may have."

The Propaganda of Woke

The pedagogical practice of having students internalize, adopt, and then articulate a particular set of beliefs not only limits the range of possible literary responses; it actually turns their literary education into a kind of propaganda. In a previous chapter I referenced English teacher Christina Torres, who coaches her students to call out the misogyny and racism in Shakespeare (Education Week, 2019). In doing so, she is dictating the content and the range of her student responses strictly and didactically as a formalist, New Critical approach might. This also veers too closely into dogmatic teaching, a kind of literary propaganda. Even if the values espoused are right and true and good, to both choose and teach texts for the sole purpose of making certain that students leave with a singular moral vision is highly problematic.

This is one of the most challenging aspects of teaching with a social justice lens. For decades, we have taught literature precisely because it is humanizing, as Atticus Finch says in the now-shunned *To Kill A Mockingbird*, to allow us to walk in other people's shoes. We want our students to be empathic and caring human beings who are invested in the dignity of all. We want them to become responsible citizens, to help ensure that the word that we will inhabit together is just and good. What right do we have to hold the literature we read hostage to a social and political goal? What do we call that kind of curriculum when we find it, often state-sponsored, in other countries?

Literature is a reflection of human experience. It reveals, mirrors, portrays, and sometimes celebrates but sometimes interrogates the sociocultural context in which the writer is embedded. Unfortunately, the woke wave tends to submerge, to drown out considerations of historical context with a kind of politically correct presentism that gives rise to anachronistic critique. Jacobs (2020) addresses this tendency as a negative factor of current literary study:

> We should judge characters of our own time, according to whether we think their behavior is good or bad, vicious or virtuous . . . . My problem with the disregard of the past that we typically manifest today is that we are highly selective in what elements of a historical person's character we are willing to take seriously. We tend to consider only those elements that reflect the dominant concerns of the moment, which are not the only concerns that are relevant to human judgment. (p. 51)

To be clear, Jacobs is not saying that we shouldn't bring our moral compasses into the reading of a text. He argues that we should, but we should do it in a nuanced way. As he says, "We need to keep *all* of our values in play, not just *some* of them" (p. 44, his emphasis).

Teaching Literature in the Era of Wokeness: Some Alternative Approaches

More than one way to respond to a text

As Wayne Booth (1988) warns, there is a kind of doctrinal criticism that can limit the range of a reader's response. This is precisely the danger of some kinds of social justice curricula. In them there is an a priori interpretive destination to which all readers are expected to arrive. To reduce a text to a particular set of modern moral values is not only a reductive reading of the text; it also limits a reader's range of response. This is concerning indeed for literary scholars who have posited for decades that, unlike the formalist New Critics before them, there is more than one way to respond to a literary text. It seems ironic that what is imperiled here is the progressive approach of encouraging multiple responses from readers, a kind of literary progressivism rooted in the progressive education philosophy of John Dewey (1997) and refined by literary scholars such as Louise Rosenblatt (1938). In other words, it seems as if progressive educators are working against the progressive, constructivist idea of multiple responses to texts in favor of strict, singular, predetermined readings, no more flexible than what the formalists prescribed.

In my own work on literary response (Appleman, 2015), I have advocated for the interpretive strategy of reading texts from multiple critical lenses, to offer both the ability to read and to respond to texts from a variety of perspectives. Critical theory also provides an interpretive tool to help readers learn to read and resist the ideologies that are inscribed in texts, often as a sometimes unconscious reflection of the worldview and perspective of the author and his or her sociocultural and historical context. As Heidi Stevens (2021) asserts,

It is undeniable progress when we start to examine the books and movies and other works of art we collectively digest, the statues that dot our public lands, the names of schools that educate our children through more than one lens. Through not just the lens of the creator at the time of creation, or the group with the most power or the group with the loudest voices. . . . But through the lens, also, of the people affected—and too often harmed—by the thing we're discussing. More lenses get us closer to the truth. More lenses broaden and deepen our understanding of who we are and who we want to become; who's been heard and who's been harmed. (paras. 10, 14)

Rather than simply not reading texts that offend, this is the kind of work that can actually help students learn lessons from them. What lessons do they learn when something is banned, when someone else determined for them that a text was unfit to read? By insisting on reading literary texts from the exclusive lens of social justice, teachers are shutting down or eliminating all other possible readings of a text.

The value of reevaluating, one text at a time

As I argue throughout this book, more is lost than gained in our students' education and our cultural maps when we choose to ban texts rather than to trouble them. While there clearly may be texts that are unfit for classroom consumption, this is generally not the case for the texts that are being called out, canceled, or banned. In some sense, refusing to teach them is the easiest way out.

Let's consider each text, each case one at time, thinking carefully through what it might contribute, what it reveals about the evolution of our social thinking and moral behavior. Let's take each text and weigh its original intent and context. Let's remember that reading anything doesn't mean that we are endorsing the values we find within it. Let's recommit ourselves to a kind of literary education that understands that literature is indeed the mirror of human experience, both for good and for ill. Literature can carry the reader to many unexpected places. Our role as teachers of literature is to not predetermine their destination.

A False Choice

It seems that the battle lines have been drawn. On one side are defenders of the great books of the Western canon. On the other are proponents of a more inclusive curriculum: one that directly challenges the white supremacy inherent in a Eurocentric curriculum that reifies power dynamics and continues to marginalize BIPOC groups by either exclusion or mischaracterization. Thus, the literature diet as assigned by literature teachers would either be (1) the staid and troublesome canon with some compelling yet flawed invitations to other worlds, other perspectives, and other times or (2) a contemporary and relevant set of texts curated on a fairly narrow definition of what might resonate with and validate the experiences and identities of contemporary adolescents. Chapter 5 examines this conundrum—what I regard as a false choice—in more detail.

Troubled Texts: To Teach or Not to Teach

We may exhort ourselves to read tolerantly, we may quote Coleridge on the willing suspension of disbelief until we think ourselves totally suspended in a relativistic universe, and still we will find many books which postulate readers we refuse to become, books that depend on "beliefs" or "attitudes" . . . which we cannot adopt even hypothetically as our own.

—WAYNE BOOTH

Over the past decade, with acceleration over the last couple of years, scores of books and other texts have been troubled out of existence, leaving the high school literature curriculum bereft of many staples and anchor texts. Calls for the addition of trigger warnings as a required prelude to novel study have become increasingly common. So, too, have been demands to remove certain literary texts from classrooms, as the new wave of cancel culture subjects both authors and material to renewed scrutiny, with an increasingly challenging and sometimes unpredictable set of criteria for appropriateness. As we have seen, even Shakespeare has come under attack because of accusations of excessive violence, misogyny, racism, and anti-Semitism, among other charges. To be sure, the standard fare of high school literature classes has remained frighteningly and discouragingly stable for the last few decades. In fact, the list of the most commonly taught texts, originally complied by Arthur Applebee, (1993) has barely changed since the middle of the last century:

1. *Romeo and Juliet* by Shakespeare
2. *Macbeth* by Shakespeare
3. *Huckleberry Finn* by Mark Twain
4. *Julius Caesar* by Shakespeare
5. *To Kill a Mockingbird* by Harper Lee
6. *The Scarlet Letter* by Nathaniel Hawthorne
7. *Of Mice and Men* by John Steinbeck
8. *Hamlet* by Shakespeare
9. *The Great Gatsby* by F. Scott Fitzgerald
10. *Lord of the Flies* by William Golding

A more recent survey by Stallworth and Gibbons (2012) noted the appearance of a few more diverse texts as well as texts by women authors but found the list to be remarkably consistent with previous surveys. Novels such as *Adventures of Huckleberry Finn, To Kill a Mockingbird, Catcher in the Rye, Of Mice and Men,* and the Shakespeare plays *Hamlet* and *Romeo and Juliet* have been perennial staples of the high school literature curriculum for decades.

I want to be clear that in many ways, troubling the traditional high school canon is good and necessary; it is an opportunity to hear previously unheard voices and to reappraise the curriculum. It is certainly true that the high school curriculum is in woeful need of revision. I have long advocated for revising this relatively staid and static list to be more inclusive of diverse voices and emerging authors and more responsive to the changing nature of contemporary adolescence and the sociocultural context of schools. What I didn't expect was that this change would occur by abrupt and sometimes seemingly arbitrary cancellation, rather than by intentional curricular design grounded in sound pedagogical theory as well as understanding of the changing literary and social landscapes.

A case in point recently occurred in Burbank, California, where five novels had been challenged: Harper

Lee's *To Kill a Mockingbird*, Mark Twain's *Adventures of Huckleberry Finn*, John Steinbeck's *Of Mice and Men*, Theodore Taylor's *The Cay*, and Mildred D. Taylor's New-bery Medal–winning young adult classic, *Roll of Thunder, Hear My Cry*. According to a local Burbank paper (Pineda, 2020), "The challenges came from four parents (three of them Black) for alleged potential harm to the public school district's roughly 400 Black students. All but *Huckleberry Finn* have been required reading in the BUSD."

Interestingly, it is not only the traditional fare of the secondary literature curriculum that has come under fire. Canonical texts are not the only ones that are susceptible to this serious and significant wave of scrutiny. Some relative newcomers to the literature curriculum have also been subject to cancellation by both conservative critics as well as progressive educators. Authors relatively new (and welcome) to the secondary literature curriculum such as Toni Morrison have been canceled, in Morrison's case because of potentially triggering subject matter such as incest in *The Bluest Eye*. Other authors, such as Sherman Alexie and Junot Díaz, as we discussed in Chapter 2, have been canceled because of revelations and accusations about their personal conduct, spurring judgments about their character or moral behavior that have nothing to do with either the content or quality of the book under question. Young adult novels and their authors have been targeted in two major ways—potentially triggering subject matter and author behavior. A list of potentially problematic young adult novels lists 341 novels as well as more than 40 different kinds of possible triggering content (Hannah, n.d.). Ironically, the very genre that is frequently lauded as being relevant and even helpful to adolescents as they face significant psychological and emotional challenges has been labeled as unteachable because of those very subjects. In addition to issues of the subject of the novels, as I discussed in Chapter 2, there have been a slew of incidents of young adult authors such as Kosoko Jackson and Amelie Wen Zhao who have been censured even before their books come to publication,

Still other texts, both classic and contemporary, are subject to a kind of revisionist reappraisal, as contemporary standards of equity (at best) and political correctness (at worst) raise issues of language and character portrayals so problematic that the texts are rendered unteachable. One of the issues at play here is our inability or failure to offer historical contexts for texts. Or, as Dorany Pineda (2020) puts it, how to teach old books in new times.

Take, for example, the case of Shylock in *The Merchant of Venice*. I had a heated argument with a colleague when

I was teaching the play. As a fellow Jew, he couldn't understand how I could be willing to teach the play given what is widely viewed as a largely anti-Semitic portrait. While there is certainly some evidence that supports that even within the context of Shakespeare's time, there was some clearly anti-Jewish sentiment, those who point to Shylock's occupation as a usurer as evidence of anti-Semitic caricature miss an important historical point. Jews were not allowed to own land and had limited occupations available to them. Shakespeare's choice to cast Shylock as a usurer was most likely dictated by the economic realities of the time. To superimpose the rules and implications of contemporary society to a different historical context is foolhardy at best and misleading at worst.

For all of these reasons—inappropriate language, questionable moral conduct of the author, insensitive portrayal of women and other groups, the transmission of a problematic set of beliefs about the world, disturbing subject matter, perpetuated stereotypes—these texts have been rendered unteachable. But are they?

The teaching of literature has always been about more than the texts themselves. In the site of learning that literature provides, we learn about habits of mind, about critical thinking, and about the very nature of the human experience. Yes, we learn about values, which is not the same as didactically teaching them or inculcating them, regardless of whether they originate from the left or the right of the political spectrum.

In this new era of culture wars, it seems as if the profession of literacy educators has offered two opposite and equally problematic responses to the challenges of the high school literature curriculum. Many texts have simply been removed from the library shelves, from classrooms, and from the curriculum. This solution of dealing with these troublesome texts is to silence them by drumming them out of existence. Some of the texts, rather than being banned completely, have become fodder for a particular kind of rereading (the #DisruptTexts approach). As discussed in Chapter 4, while there are certainly some merits to this approach, there are also considerable dangers. It can lead of an oversimplification of texts, making them merely a foil to make a historical point. Ironically, it can easily become just as didactic and closed as an unreflective traditional curriculum could be. Perhaps there is a better way to deal with troublesome texts rather than make the books completely disappear or turn them into fodder for commentary about their political incorrectness.

Literature teachers don't want to engage in harm by offering, in an untroubled or uncritical fashion, attitudes and racist and sexist tropes that harm students and complicitly acquiesce or worse, support those attitudes. Certainly there may be some material that is so objectionable it has no place in the high school curriculum. This could be because of its depictions of violence, gratuitous use of sex, excessive vulgar language, or hateful attitudes toward particular groups. (I purposely refrain here from citing specific texts, since unacceptability is so dependent on context including student characteristics and community standards.)

As I have argued elsewhere (Appleman, 2015), literary study can help our students learn to read and resist ideology—a central purpose that in the 21st century has never been more important. Literature provides a site of inquiry like no other for exploring the human condition. As part of that exploration, we can help students learn to read both texts and worlds with a nuanced and critical eye. We can teach them to discover how power and privilege are inscribed all around us so they can become the enlightened witnesses that bell hooks (1994) called for and that we so desperately need in these particularly troubled times. Perhaps this means that we interrogate the abuse of power and privilege of now-shunned authors like Alexie. Doing so may mean we need to raise the question by engaging in the work, rather than removing it from the curriculum.

What follows are some suggestions to offer teachers of literature at both the high school and the college level a more nuanced approach to this current, powerful reappraisal of how and what we teach.

Teaching Literature in the New Culture Wars: Some Alternative Approaches

Teaching the controversy or teaching the conflict

The first and perhaps most direct approach is to teach the controversy, as Gerald Graff famously discussed. In *Beyond the Culture Wars: How Teaching the Conflicts Can Revitalize American Education* (1993), Graff presciently discusses the culture wars and their divisive influence on literary study. He argues that rather than avoid particular points of contention, "intellectual conflict should be made part of the universities' object of study and thereby more successfully engaging students in the world of ideas and learning":

> In recent writings, I have been proposing a solution to these conflicts that I think is both practical and democratic: teach them. My argument is that the most educationally effective way to deal with present conflicts

over education and culture is to teach the conflicts themselves. (p. 57)

To be sure, the kinds of conflicts Graff was addressing nearly three decades ago were different in some significant ways from the current issues of triggers and cancel culture. His focus was primarily on the university culture and curriculum. Still, his primary point about facing the conflicts and incorporating them into the curriculum, rather than ignoring them, seems particularly relevant for this new iteration of the culture wars.

Graff's exhortation to teach the conflicts, while originally designed for the university classroom and curriculum, can be profitably integrated into secondary literature and humanities classrooms. Specifically, secondary students could be presented with the conflict, whether it is about unsettling revelations about the character of the author, revised sensibilities about language, or hard fought and critical realizations about the ways in which certain people are portrayed. The values and social norms that are presented or represented in the text can also be discussed and interrogated.

The strength of this approach is that it offers two sides to an issue about a text, rather than deciding a priori where the argument would land. Skeptics of this strategy might rightly argue that there are not, or should not be, two sides to certain issues— no opposing view, for example, in the condemnation of racism, misogyny, and homophobia. Yet in this context, the conflict is not about the attitudes that are animated, often offensively in the texts themselves; the conflict is about the value of learning from points of view that are different from our own, considering the evolution of social thought and positions and considering the ways in which a piece of literature reflects not necessarily the times in which it is read but rather the times in which it is written. As Heidi Stevens (2021) writes, "It's a welcome evolution—a necessary one, even—to revisit the things and the people and the virtues held dear by tastemakers whose tastes weren't shared, or informed by, the people they harmed."

Graff's approach (1993) offers a middle ground between the past practice of presenting the classics almost reverently and the current practice of removing them from the curriculum entirely. For example, he writes: "Had I been exposed to a little 'disrespect' for the classics, I might have found studying them more rewarding than I did." What might this strategy look like in the high school literature classroom? There are many materials discussing the controversy surrounding *Adventures of Huckleberry Finn* that students could read and discuss, including the film *Born to Trouble* (2000), which chronicles the controversy that occurred in an Arizona high school when the novel was taught. Offering students the opportunity to read the novel and discuss its appropriateness for their literary education can sharpen students' critical thinking skills, and help them develop aesthetic sensibilities by discussing the relative literary value of the work. In addition, teachers can invite students to consider the complex issues of race, discuss the implications of using the n-word, and discuss what kinds of texts should be studied in school and why. In other words, why not let students discuss the controversy themselves, rather than not teach the book at all?

Critical Lenses

Literary theory can be used to trouble troubled texts by introducing students to critical lenses that accompany their reading of a literary text (Appleman, 2015). Critical lenses provide an interpretive frame to consider the ideologies that drive the text and to question and—when necessary—resist them. They provide students with multiple perspectives on a text, something that neither untroubled traditional presentation nor one-sided attacks on the texts can provide. I think of lenses as a kind of ideological corrective, a way of laying bare the assumptions that undergird the text, the author, the world that is represented in the text, and the world in which the text was produced. Rather than ban texts completely because of their problematic assumptions, why not read critically so that the students might interrogate those assumptions and have an opportunity for critical analysis?

Ironically, my first foray into teaching critical lenses was created by a challenge I faced in teaching *Lolita* to a high school student who had chosen that novel as an independent reading (Appleman, 1993). Even though I hadn't sponsored or promoted or assigned the reading, I felt uncomfortable having her read the novel in an uncritical way. We read feminist theory as we read the novel, which offered the student an opportunity to not only read the text but also to question it on her own with her reading of the text. Similar to the current tendency to eliminate or cancel certain reading material, my initial instinct was to not have her read the book. Instead, I trusted her to read it but also gave her the supplementary materials that would enable her to critique it. The opportunity to both read and simultaneously critique the text using the lens of contemporary feminist theory proved to be a positive and fruitful approach for the student, one that I later amplified in *Critical Encounters in Secondary*

English: Teaching Literary Theory to Adolescents (2015). In that work, I have explicated the ways in which a variety of theoretical frames or lenses can be used to explore texts—reader response, formalist, postcolonial, class or Marxist, and gender or feminist.

Perhaps a multiple theoretical approach, especially if critical race theory is used, can be seen as being related to the #DisruptTexts movement. Yet there are some very important differences between these approaches, differences that perhaps get to the heart of the matter with the culture wars. Critical thinking and open-mindedness will not be encouraged by replacing one monolithic perspective with another, leaving little room for nuance or variety in student interpretation. The primary objective of using critical lenses is to offer multiple theoretical perspectives, in part to offset the charge—a central claim against critical race theory—that students are being indoctrinated or brainwashed.

Unmooring Anchor Texts

Part of the issue with canonical texts that have been challenged has been the lack of student choice; in addition to the texts being offensive, they were required reading. Perhaps part of the solution is simply not to require them, but still make them available as a choice. Student choice is another possible approach to teaching or not teaching troubled or troubling texts. One of the challenges that teachers especially at the secondary level have is to assign one text to all students, regardless of their experiences, identity, or positionality. One of the first challenges that some secondary teachers have faced with regard to this has been with the teaching of the staple *To Kill a Mockingbird.* Different students and their parents respond in various ways to the teaching of a text with the presence of the n-word, a familiar scenario with *Adventures of Huckleberry Finn* as well. Part of the issue, of course, is when the curriculum requires that every student read the book. What if there are other texts the students could choose? Of course, that doesn't ameliorate the problematic and troubling aspects of the text itself, but it does offer opportunities to honor student choice without completely removing the text from the curriculum.

Pairing texts

To expand this notion of decentering troublesome anchor texts, in addition to not requiring that all students read the same text, what if the offending or troubled texts were paired with texts that completely called the other text into question, by virtue of its perspective, author, or point of view?

Pairing texts allows for a rich intertextual dialogue. It becomes a kind of literary call and response. For example, one could pair *Adventures of Huckleberry Finn* with *Incidents in the Life of a Slave Girl* or *The Absolutely True Diary of a Part-Time Indian*. Or *Catcher in the Rye* with *Prep, 1984,* and *Feed; Romeo and Juliet* and *The Fault in Our Stars* or *To Kill a Mockingbird* with *Just Mercy.* This last suggested pairing raises another idea, pairing novels with nonfiction, including nonfiction texts that offer some empirical perspectives on some of the assumptions or portrayals in the text that might be problematic. The objective behind a paired novel approach is that the novel doesn't stand by itself uninterrupted and untroubled. The intertextual nature of the students' reading experience helps raise important issues and calls attention to problems within the text.

Another version of decentering a troublesome novel, a version that has become increasingly popular, is the text set. This is an approach that works well with readers at any grade level. A text set usually includes shorter pieces, such as short stories, poems, and several nonfiction pieces. A text set can frame and contextualize a troubling text. Some of the pieces that could be included in the text set could be works that directly challenge or take on the text in question. Partly in response to the common core state standards adopted by most school systems, many ELA (English Language Arts) teachers sought ways to incorporate nonfiction into their curriculum. Texts sets can offer a way to do just that, and material that contradicts, enlightens, or expands the text can be incorporated into literary study.

What we stand to lose

In the Burbank, California case discussed at the beginning of this chapter, one high school student lamented the removal of *Roll of Thunder, Hear My Cry* and began a petition to have the book reinstated: "I didn't know much about race relations or anything regarding critical race theory when I was younger," he said, "and when I read *Roll of Thunder, Hear My Cry*, that was my first glimpse, and it really did touch me." He hopes students can continue to have the "breakthrough moment" he did (Pineda, 2021).

Similarly, a high school educator (Hoover, 2021) weighed in on the critical race theory debate by reminding us of the competence and ability of her students:

This is one reason why I get so frustrated at all the bad

takes circulating among politicians, social media, and the news related to critical race theory and the teaching of America's racial history in K–12 classrooms. The reality is that kids are talking about race, systems of oppression, and our country's ugly past anyway— from media coverage to last summer's protests to even this very controversy itself, my students are absorbing these conversations and want to know more. I'm just one teacher, and there's no way to generalize what's happening everywhere. But I believe that my students are smart and mature enough to handle the truth. (para. 3)

I worry about what this latest rash of book cancellations teaches students. Whether the cancellations are politically motivated or motivated by sincere concerns for the well-being of students, the kinds of absolute judgments that are rendered are unforgiving and decontextualized. In addition, these cancellations can serve as a powerful model of the kind of cancel culture that some adolescents themselves have experienced. While teaching about social justice is laudable, how do students learn to engage and effectively oppose contrasting perspectives if they are not even allowed in the classroom? By removing these texts from the curriculum, we are removing the opportunity for students to do critical analysis.

We need to do more than remove troubled texts from the secondary literature curriculum. We need to trust our students and ourselves to teach them, to trouble them, and to engage in the kind of rigorous intellectual and aesthetic debate that is a critical part of literary study.

CHAPTER 6

Conclusion: Teaching Literature and the New Culture Wars

You think your pain and your heartbreak are unprecedented in the history of the world, but then you read. It was books that taught me that the things that tormented me most were the very things that connected me with all the people who were alive, or who had ever been alive.

—JAMES BALDWIN

These are indeed troubling times. As I write, the world is slowly and cautiously reawakening from a global pandemic, a shuttering and withdrawal that has forced a rethinking of many of our bedrock social institutions, including schooling at all levels. The basic elements of schooling, the rhythm and dynamics of the classroom, so familiar that we took them for granted, were no longer possible. Remote learning has disrupted many of our educational norms, as traditional ways of teaching and discussing texts became impossible. In many cases, this disruption prompted necessary and healthy reappraisals of what we should be teaching and how we should be teaching it. Although there were clearly some significant technological and pedagogical developments that led to positive learning, most students and teachers, from kindergarten through graduate school, had an extremely challenging eighteen months of schooling. We were all on edge, teachers and students alike, and none of us had our best selves show up to our virtual classrooms. Perhaps that generalized edginess contributed to the bitterness of this most recent iteration of the complex and confounding culture wars in which we currently find ourselves.

In addition to the myriad of difficulties caused by the pandemic, there was another dramatic kind of social upheaval as well. I write these words from the Twin Cities of Minneapolis/St. Paul, scant miles away from the site of the murder of George Floyd in May of 2020. I write from the epicenter of an event that taught us all the most brutal and heartbreaking of lessons, that business as usual had to be stopped—on our streets, in our neighborhoods, and, of course, in our schools. This incident spurred, on a global scale, a radical and much needed racial reawakening, one that undeniably added urgency to the increasingly strident calls for a more racially sensitive and socially just literature curriculum.

This radical racial reawaking is only part of our current political, psychological, sociological, and educational landscape. In the United States, we find ourselves in a country that is bitterly divided along political lines, in ways that seem more defined and more antagonistic than ever before. We seem to have moved beyond the divisions of political parties into a kind of cultural tribalism that views contradictory opinions as ignorance, even heresy. Even the question of whether students should be required to wear masks in school or receive vaccinations created bitter divisions among parents of school children, administrators, and even governors. In this atmosphere, having a nuanced and informed discussion about something as potentially volatile as critical race theory seems nearly impossible.

All of these factors—economic uncertainty, fear for well-being in the face of a ravaging pandemic, heightened racial sensitivity, and fiercely held political positions have contributed to the fomenting of the kinds of culture wars that have led to the concerns that are addressed in this book—triggers, cancel culture, and a narrow and limiting focus on a kind of extreme version of political correctness or so-called wokeness. All these elements are brought to bear in our classrooms and influence this new era of teaching texts in these troubling times.

This final chapter argues for a reasoned approach to determine what literature still deserves to be read and taught and discussed, despite some troubling characteristics. It calls for a refocusing of the intellectual and affective work that literature can do and argues that there are ways to continue to teach troubling texts without doing harm.

What Makes a Text Troubling?

As we have discussed throughout this book, there are several considerations that cause a text to be troubling or problematic in ways that may render it unteachable in these difficult times. The first is the content of the text itself. Both classic and contemporary texts face a renewed level of scrutiny with regard to the kinds of social attitudes and beliefs the text animates, through either the unconscious endorsement that comes from unawareness or from a more overt and conscious portrayal that is congruent with certain social beliefs such as the place of women in society or the stereotyped and often demeaning portrayals of marginalized people and cultures. Sometimes, this scrutiny of textual content is specifically centered around the language used by the text, especially the use of the n-word, which has rendered unteachable some of the classic staples of the American secondary literature curriculum. Works by authors of color, such as James Baldwin, Toni Morrison, and Richard Wright have not been immune from such censure as well, both because of considerations of language and topics such as incest, infanticide, and other forms of violence.

In addition to particular textual properties, whether the concerns are about language or content, some books have become problematic because of some issue or concern about the author, concerns that are not directly related to the text itself. These authorial concerns have implicated current living authors as well as deceased literary figures, established literary luminaries and emerging new literary talent. Troubling revelations about the author that lead to a negative reappraisal of the teachability of a particular text vary in nature from comments that the author may make in decontextualized settings, as in the case of J. K. Rowling's Twitter feed or discoveries or accusations about inappropriate behavior, as is the case with Sherman Alexie, Junot Díaz, and others. This category of scrutiny and censure differs significantly from the first because it is not the text itself that is deemed problematic; instead, non-literary-based scrutiny about the author renders a particular work unteachable, even works that have been admired for both their literary merit and their pedagogical value.

Of course, there have always been troubling and problematic texts, texts that have been censored or judged inappropriate for public school classrooms because they contain sensitive, even objectionable content, or offensive and anachronistic portrayals of people or whole cultures. In the past, teachers often performed their own individual calculus of whether a text should be taught. They evaluated the teachability of texts based on a wide array of student characteristics, the specific properties of the text, including subject matter, use of language, underlying issues, and overall perspective and context, including the relationship of the subject matter to current social and political issues. They made specific and contextualized decisions based on the text, the teaching context, and, most important, their students. In these troubling times, however, it seems what was once, for better or worse, the province of individual pedagogical prerogative is now, as Anne Applebaum (2021) suggests, in the court of public opinion at best and mob mentality at worst.

To be sure, as I have emphasized throughout this book, there is some inarguable value to the heightened awareness and increased scrutiny to particular texts. Content such as characterizations and racist and misogynist tropes found within the pages of some previously lauded texts have rendered them intolerable, so troublesome that they should no longer be taught. In these cases, it is not sufficient to merely ignore the controversy or to dismiss serious and sustained objections to the work or calls for the work to be removed from the curriculum. Silence is acquiescence, an implicit acceptance of problematic portrayals and attitudes. Speaking out against and working to disrupt behavior and attitudes that demean and oppress others is what all educators should be doing. Texts that reproduce harmful social attitudes need to be interrogated, disrupted, and resisted. Clearly there are some texts that should no longer be taught; their historical place on the secondary literature curriculum can no longer be justified as we weigh their assumed literary value and aesthetic significance against the harm they might possibly do by perpetuating unacceptable social attitudes and anachronistic beliefs. These texts simply are not deserving of our students' attention. To put it more strongly, they are too potentially harmful to be taught. In this regard, the work of activist educator collectives such as #DisruptTexts has been invaluable in their bold efforts to raise these important questions and increase the awareness of educators about the troublesome nature of certain texts.

Triggers Revisited

There are other factors to consider as we reappraise the teaching of troublesome texts in these troubling times. In addition to considering the potentially problematic content of a text as well as the biography, positionality, and conduct of the author, it is also imperative to consider our students' identities in all their complexities—their experience, sensitivities, and vulnerabilities. Some texts that might not be problematic in one context become troublesome in another.

Considering the social, psychological, and emotional state of students both individually and as a collective community of learners may cause teachers to reconsider the relative appropriateness of a text in specific classroom situations. A necessary reappraisal might arise, for example, when a suicide occurs in a school. For example, as a high school teacher, a student's suicide made me pull several pieces from my curriculum, including *Ordinary People* by Judith Guest and "Richard Cory" by Edwin Arlington Robinson.

I maintain that these kinds of careful considerations are very different from the generalized approach to trigger warnings that I discussed in Chapter 3. Considering the sociocultural context and positionalities of students when considering the teachability of a text offers a more nuanced approach than simply asserting a priori that a particular text is triggering. In one case, it is a real-time response to a specific situation. In the other, it is an assumption of vulnerability, a generalized set of assumptions about the nature of the text and a response it might elicit in readers. As Khalid and Snyder (2021) write in an op-ed about trigger warnings published in *The Chronicle of Higher Education*,

> As it happens, the distribution of trigger warnings by topic often seems arbitrary. Suicide, sexual assault, and eating disorders typically make the cut. Warfare, cancer, and starving children do not. We don't think we have the expertise or moral authority to make decisions about what kind of pain—not to mention whose pain—matters most. Indeed, we're skeptical that anyone does. (para. 22)

Our overuse of trigger warnings also makes some erroneous assumptions about how triggers work. Recent research is pretty clear that trigger warnings don't work, at least not in the way they were intended to. In fact, the use of trigger warnings can actually work against the kind of engagement with texts that we seek in our literature classes. Khalid and Snyder (2021) make this case clearly:

> It seems unavoidable that policies like these would impede meaningful engagement with difficult top-ics and reinforce the idea that students are inherently fragile. Indeed, embracing trigger warnings may drive some students to be on high alert for any content that might possibly upset or offend. (para. 16)

Critical Race Theory Revisited: A Case Study of the New Culture Wars

The deep anxieties and social fissures we are experiencing as a nation are animated in our schools, as a new wave of culture wars floods our consideration of what we teach and why as well as how we teach it. As Stephen Sawchuk of *Education Week* (2021) writes,

> The culture wars are always, at some level, battled out within schools, historians say. "It's because they're nervous about broad social things, but they're talking

in the language of school and school curriculum," said one historian of education. "That's the vocabulary, but grammar is anxiety about shifting social power relations." (paras. 40–41)

This is precisely the reason why the teaching of critical race theory (CRT) has become a particularly dramatic flashpoint. This is why, as I discussed in Chapter 5, I have hesitated about including critical race theory as one of the critical lenses in my work with students on literary theory. The teaching of critical race theory, a theoretical framework originally grounded in law and social science, has become a particularly contentious skirmish in this new wave of culture wars. As educator Jania Hoover (2021) states, "Certain state legislators and pundits . . . have manufactured a crisis surrounding CRT precisely because most people do not know what it is. The goal is to scare parents, who will then scare teachers away from discussing an accurate representation of past events in the US."

This specific controversy is worth further examination because it is an example of the kinds of polarization and misunderstandings that characterize the new culture wars. The controversy is, I think, both overblown and ill-informed. First, there are very few teachers at the secondary level (and almost none at the primary level) who actually teach the tenets of critical race theory. Hoover (2021) explains:

> Most of the people discussing critical race theory aren't really discussing the theory itself, which is something taught in some law schools, but not—as far as I know—in most or any K–12 schools. Instead, what these critics seem to be talking about is a brain dump of unrelated buzzwords related to hot button topics in society, such as racism, privilege, diversity, equity, and inclusion. (para. 5)

Second, critical race theory has been deeply misunderstood, ironically not only by those who oppose it but even by some who espouse it. It has not been a part of our teacher education, woven into our pedagogical content knowledge. In efforts to apply the basic tenets of CRT to traditional school disciplines such as social studies or language arts, its original structure and intent sometimes gets lost in translation.

Third, the objections to teaching critical race theory may seem hyperbolic and without any empirical grounding. For example, critics of CRT claim that correcting historical records means they will be distorted, twisted into unrecognizable form. Critics also worry that the primary message of critical race theory is that white people are evil and despicable. Parents worry that this anti-white discourse will negatively affect white students and lead to damaging negative self-images. Stephen Sawchuk (2021) explains:

> As with CRT in general, its popular representation in schools has been far less nuanced. A recent poll by the advocacy group Parents Defending Education claimed some schools were teaching that "white people are inherently privileged, while Black and other people of color are inherently oppressed and victimized"; that "achieving racial justice and equality between racial groups requires discriminating against people based on their whiteness"; and that "the United States was founded on racism." (para. 25)

Because of these frenzied fears, there even is legislation designed to ban CRT from schools in several states. Despite the furor, many seasoned educators have articulated solid reasons to include critical race theory in their curricula. Social studies educator Jania Hoover (2021) comments:

- The unsavory realities of US history will not teach [students] to hate this country.
- I also believe that we do not help kids by lying to them. Telling them the truth about how our country was built makes kids appreciate me more.
- There's also value in teaching kids to evaluate information from multiple perspectives—it makes them better at every aspect of life.

Some teachers simply assert that they don't want their students to be lied to about the past. As part of the Zinn Education Project (2021), thousands of teachers signed a pledge to teach history honestly, in part as a response to the legislation to ban CRT from the classroom. Here is the pledge they signed:

> "One has not only a legal, but a moral responsibility to obey just laws. Conversely, one has a moral responsibility to disobey unjust laws."—Martin Luther King Jr. ("Letter From Birmingham Jail," April 1963). We, the undersigned educators, refuse to lie to young people about US history and current events. (para. 9)

It's difficult to imagine how to teach history as well as many literary texts without being able to mention the structure and effect of race and racism. How, for example, could teachers begin to approach topics like slavery, the Civil War, Jim Crow, or the Civil Rights Movement without discussing race? How can one teach the works of James Baldwin, Richard Wright, Toni Morrison, Jimmy Santiago Baca, Sandra Cisneros, and others without engaging in explicit and extended discussion about race and identity? Again, there is an issue of balance that seems missing from this debate. While a reasonable observer wouldn't want to include some authors who are accused of being racist and unteachable, this extreme kind of legislation about CRT can be seen to be silencing, muffling, and a violation of teachers' academic freedom.

Ironically, some of the same pedagogical impulses that have forwarded the notion of critical literacy are among those at the heart of the movement to silence or cancel texts. Is the controversy surrounding the teaching of critical race theory much ado about nothing, or is it perhaps an example of the ways in which we continue to misunderstand and mischaracterize each other's positions, deeply affecting what our children are learning? Are we unnecessarily stirring up a bit too much trouble by exaggerating the ideological contours and potential consequences of each other's positions?

Mob Mentality?

The kind of exaggeration and ideological frenzy surrounding critical race theory has led writer Anne Applebaum (2021) to characterize some of the responses to battles within these culture wars as a kind of mob mentality that threatens to stifle free and unfettered expression of conflicting ideas:

> This is a story of moral panic, of cultural institutions policing or purifying themselves in the face of disapproving crowds. The crowds are no longer literal, as they once were in Salem, but rather online mobs, organized via Twitter, Facebook, or sometimes internal company Slack channels. . . .
>
> [I]f we drive all of the difficult people, the demanding people, and the eccentric people away from the creative professions where they used to thrive, we will become a flatter, duller, less interesting society, a place where manuscripts sit in drawers for fear of arbitrary judgments. The arts, the humanities, and the media will become stiff, predictable, and mediocre. Democratic principles like the rule of law, the right to self-defense,

the right to a just trial—even the right to be forgiven—
will wither. There will be nothing to do but sit back
and wait for the Hawthornes of the future to expose
us. (paras. 37, 59)

Author Chimamanda Ngozi Adichie also worries about a
kind of ideological frenzy as even small personal injuries,
real or imagined, turn into all-out culture wars. Adichie
herself became a kind of target of cancel culture when a
former student and mentee took umbrage at a comment
about trans women that Adichie made in an interview.
The incident was personal, but Adichie linked it to the
hypervigilance that has led to the kinds of cancellations
of authors that I discussed in Chapter 2. Adichie is quoted
by Alexandra Atler (2021) in a *New York Times* article:

> "There are many social-media-savvy people who are
> choking on sanctimony and lacking in compassion,
> who can fluidly pontificate on Twitter about kind-
> ness but are unable to actually show kindness," she
> wrote. "People whose social media lives are case stud-
> ies in emotional aridity. People for whom friendship,
> and its expectations of loyalty and compassion and
> support, no longer matter. People who claim to love
> literature—the messy stories of our humanity—but

are also monomaniacally obsessed with whatever is the prevailing ideological orthodoxy." (para. 6)

Ironically, Adichie long ago provided one of the solutions or antidotes to these frenetically held positions, this obsession with the "prevailing ideological orthodoxy" in her plea to consider issues, controversies, human beings, and stories from more than one perspective. In a widely viewed TED talk, "The Danger of a Single Story" (2009), she warns of the dangers of looking at things from a singular point of view:

> The single story creates stereotypes, and the problem with stereotypes is not that they are untrue, but that they are incomplete. They make one story become the only story. . . . I've always felt that it is impossible to engage properly with a place or a person without engaging with all of the stories of that place and that person. The consequence of the single story is this: It robs people of dignity. It makes our recognition of our equal humanity difficult. It emphasizes how we are different rather than how we are similar.

Although it might seem simplistic, perhaps if we inhabited the perspectives of the opposition in the culture wars, the frenzy would be reduced, and we'd be able to consider both the troubling aspects and potentially redeeming qualities of texts from multiple perspectives.

Coming to Terms With the Past

To read literature also means that we come to terms with the past, in an honest, full, and uncensored way. Much of the trouble with literary texts has arisen with historical, once classic texts that portray values and beliefs that are anachronistic at best, demeaning at worst. The works of Shakespeare, Mark Twain, Hemingway, and others may fall into this category. Is the solution of their problematic portrayals not to read their works at all?

In, *Breaking Bread with the Dead* (2020), Alan Jacobs quotes L. P. Hartley: "The past is a foreign country; they do things differently there." Jacobs continues by encouraging readers to engage with the past even if it is in conflict with our current values and understandings:

> The decisions of our ancestors, however strange those people may be to us, touch us and our world; and our decisions will touch the lives of those who come after us. By understanding what moved them and what they hoped for, we give ourselves a better chance of acting wisely—in some cases, as those ancestors *did*; in

others, as they *didn't*. We judge them, as we should, as we must; but if we judge them fairly and proportionately, as we ourselves hope someday to be judged, then we may use them well with an eye toward the future. Simone Weil, as we saw, recommends studying the past because the past may sometimes be more than we are, while the future, being imagined by us, is confined by our limitations. But I do not wholly agree: *if* our imaginings of the future are grounded in a deep and sympathetic knowledge of the past, then we may have the personal density required to imagine a future that lies beyond the confines of our experience. (p. 143)

Similarly, in *Beyond the Culture Wars* (1993), Gerald Graff also takes on the issue of dealing with the past by directly engaging with it, rather than banishing those historical texts that offend us. He quotes Karl Marx on the topic:

[I]t seems unlikely that anything like a consensus on literature, culture, and the teaching of these subjects is likely to be attainable soon. Anyone who has experienced the theoretical perturbations of recent years would have had no illusions on that score. Perhaps the most interesting aspect of the current situation in the teaching of literature is in fact the extent of the differences that divide us.

Unfortunately, we do not take sufficient advantage of those differences for pedagogical purposes. Instead of sharing them with students, using them for what they are, a source of interest, vitality, and direction, we usually keep them out of the classroom, as if they were one of the profession's truly embarrassing secrets. But why conceal our disagreements? (p. 196)

Marx's words are prescient, since the combined forces of cancel culture and trigger warnings have served to keep too many troubling texts out our classrooms. As Khalid and Snyder (2021) ask us, "Why are we so afraid to acknowledge the power of academic study to provoke, destabilize, and disturb? Conflict, pain, and suffering are central elements of any serious study of the human experience."

Conclusion

To read literature is to learn to read the world in all of its complexities. The study of literature calls for a refocusing of the intellectual and affective work that literature can do and argues that there are ways to continue to teach troubling texts without doing harm. Let us consider the larger purpose of a literary education, what it is that we want students to learn from reading texts. In addition to encountering the richness of well-written literature (even though we may not be able to agree on what that is) we also want students to glean a sense of history, to understand the interplay between social context and literature, to witness the evolution of social mores and ideas, to view things from multiple perspectives, to be able to inhabit the perspective of others, to develop empathy, and to acquire some aesthetic sensibilities.

By teaching, rather than banning, troubled and challenged literature, we can help students learn to decipher the world inscribed within the texts we read together and help them read the world around them. Students can become the "enlightened witnesses" that bell hooks (1994) calls for, noting how power and privilege are inscribed all around us, and they can learn to read both texts and worlds with a nuanced and critical eye. Our students can become, with our help, truly educated in the way James Baldwin (1963) envisioned, able to critique one's own society intelligently and without fear:

> The paradox of education is precisely this—that as one begins to become conscious one begins to examine the society in which he is being educated. The purpose of education, finally, is to create in a person the ability to look at the world for himself, to make his own deci-

sions, to say to himself this is black or this is white, to decide for himself whether there is a God in heaven or not. To ask questions of the universe, and then learn to live with those questions, is the way he achieves his own identity. But no society is really anxious to have that kind of person around. What societies really, ideally, want is a citizenry which will simply obey the rules of society. If a society succeeds in this, that society is about to perish. The obligation of anyone who thinks of himself as responsible is to examine society and try to change it and to fight it—at no matter what risk. This is the only hope society has. This is the only way societies change. (p. 330–337)

Perhaps, in the end, what we need is trust in what education can and should be—trust in the reciprocal act of teaching, trust in the reciprocal act of teaching and learning, trust in the ability of teachers to navigate their students through difficult waters, and trust in the kinds of rich pedagogical strategies that we have collectively created. Perhaps, most importantly, we need to trust our students to be able to learn to read words and worlds through a critical eye. We need to trust students to be able to parse out the harmless from the harmful, to read the world for themselves, and to develop both the critical strength and emotional resilience to notice harm and to resist it—without it being kept from them by well-meaning but overvigilant teachers. Perhaps what these troubled times need is for us to continue to teach troubling texts, and trouble the ideologies inscribed therein, rather than cancel or banish them. Our students deserve no less.

FURTHER READING

Ablao, M. (2017, March 8). Why we use trigger warnings. *The Northern Light*.

Blair, E. (2021, September 30). During Banned Books Week, readers explore what it means to challenge texts. *MPR News*.

Bristow, N. K., Johnston, A., Linenthal, E. T., Pfeifer, M. J., Shine, J., & Williams, K. E. (2015, May). Trauma and trigger warnings in the history classroom: A roundtable discussion. *The American Historian*.

Carroll, E. (2016, February 26). Of mice and men and censorship. *Study.com*.

Chow, C. (2017, March 8). Trigger warnings con: Students remain silenced and schools remain sheltered. *The Northern Light*.

Dishmon, K. (2019, May 3). The exhaustive history of "cancel culture" in YA fiction. *Bookstr*.

Drake, I. (2008, Spring). Classroom simulations: Proceed with caution. *Learning for Justice*, *33*.

Faulk, F. (2015, November 27). Do trigger warnings create a safe space for students, or coddle them? *CBC Radio*.

Forna, A. (2013, August 20). Nadine Gordimer helped me see how fiction writing can illuminate reality. *The Guardian*.

Freeman, E., Herrera, B., Hurley, N., King, H., Luciano, D.,

Seitler, D., & White, P. (2014, May 29). Trigger warnings are flawed. *Inside Higher Ed*.

George, J. (2021, January 11). A lesson on critical race theory. *Human Rights Magazine, 46*(2).

Goldberg, M. (2021, September 20). The middle-aged sadness behind the cancel culture panic. *New York Times*.

Graff, G. (1991). Teach the conflicts. In D. Gless & B. Herrnstein Smith (Eds.), *The politics of liberal education* (pp. 57–74). Duke University Press.

Graham, J. (2020, August 22). Cancel culture is entering a dangerous new phase. But there is a key to getting out. *Deseret News*.

Homer, S. (2018, April 30). Sherman Alexie or how does #MeToo affect the texts we teach? *Pedagogy & American Literary Studies*.

Johnston, A. (2014, May 29). Why I'll add a trigger warning. *Inside Higher Ed*.

Kass, J. (2021, January 29). Erasing classic literature for kids. *Chicago Tribune*.

Khazan, O. (2019, March 28). The real problem with trigger warnings. *The Atlantic*.

Linker, D. (2021, September 21). Is "cancel culture" really so bad? *The Week*.

Lukianoff, G., & Haidt, J. (2015, September). The coddling of the American mind. *The Atlantic*.

Miller, L. (2020, January 31). Will the *American Dirt* fiasco change American publishing? *Slate*.

Myers, M. (2015, August 11). Saying trigger warnings "coddle the American mind" completely misses the point. *The Mary Sue.*

Natbony, R. (n.d.). 10 successful literature pairings (modern books and classic works). *Prestwick House Blog.*

National Council of Teachers of English (NCTE). (2019, July 6). Key aspects of critical literacy: An excerpt. *Literacy & NCTE.*

Orwell, G. Why I write. In *Collected essays* (Vol. 1, p. 4).

Pabdoo. (n.d.). An introduction to content warnings and trigger warnings. *Inclusive Teaching at U-M.*

Porosoff, L. (2018, March 2). Why I'll never teach this powerful book again. *Learning for Justice.*

Scales, J. (2017, September). Banned: Of mice and men [Personal communication].

Schlosser, E. (2015, June 3). I'm a liberal professor and my liberal students terrify me. *Vox.*

Schuessler, J., & Harris, E. A. (2020, July 7). Artists and writers warn of an "intolerant climate." Reaction is swift. *New York Times.*

Schwartz, K. (2020, January 5). How the #DisruptTexts movement can help English teachers be more inclusive. *KQED.*

Shute, L. T. (2019, July 18). Writing in the age of cancel culture. https://medium.com/@laurentaylorshute/writing-in-the-age-of-cancel-culture-945b7997828d

Simmons, A. (2016, April 5). Literature's emotional lessons. *The Atlantic.*

Smith, K. (2014). Warning: This course may cause emotional distress. *American Psychological Association, 45*(7), 58.

Stanford Teacher Education Program Secondary Teaching Seminar. (2020).

Tanskanen, E. M. (2020, October 13). Cancel culture—The good, the bad, and The ugly. *Risky Networks*.

Ullman, T. (2020, August 17). Cancel culture is undermining learning and harming students like me. *FEE Stories*.

Wallace-Wells, B. (2021, March 11). Cancel culture is not a movement. *The New Yorker*.

Worth, R. (2020, July 8). The authors signing the open letter against "cancel culture" are missing the point. https:// rikcw .medium .com/the -authors -signing -the -open -letter -against -cancel -culture -are -missing -the -point -463636547d57

REFERENCES

A letter on justice and open debate. (2020, July 7). *Harper's Magazine*.

American Association of University Professors (AAUP). (2014). *On trigger warnings*. American Association of University Professors.

Adichie, C. N. (2009, July). *The danger of a single story* [TedTalk].

Alexie, S. (2003, April 21). What you pawn, I will redeem. *The New Yorker*.

Alter, A. (2018, March 27). Canceled deals and pulped books, as the publishing industry confronts sexual harassment. *New York Times*.

Alter, A. (2021, June 16). Chimamanda Ngozi Adichie sparks controversy in online essay. *New York Times*.

Alter, R. (2020, February 7). Why is everyone arguing about the novel American Dirt? *Vulture*.

American Library Association. (2021, April 5). *Top ten most challenged books of 2020*.

American Psychological Association (APA). (2017). Does research support classroom trigger warnings? *American Psychological Association*.

Applebaum, A. (2021, August 31). The new Puritans. *The Atlantic*.

Applebee, A. (1993). *Literature in the secondary school: Stud-*

ies of curriculum and instruction in the United States. National Council of Teachers of English.

Appleman, D. (1999). Alice, Lolita, and me: Learning to read 'feminist' with a tenth-grade urban adolescent. In L. B. Alvine & L. E. Cullum (Eds.), *Breaking the cycle: gender, literacy, and learning,* Heinemann, 71–88.

Appleman, D. (1993). Looking through critical lenses: Teaching literary theory to secondary students. In S. Straw & D. Bogdan (Eds.), *Constructive reading: Teaching beyond communication.* Boynton/Cook.

Appleman, D. (2015). *Critical encounters in secondary English* (3rd ed.). Teachers College Press.

Baculi, S. (2020, December 5). YA author Jessica Cluess denounced and dropped by agent for "personal attacks" against Lorena German. *Bounding into Comics.*

Baldwin J. (1963, October 16). A talk to teachers. *The Saturday Review.*

Baldwin, J. (1963, May 24). The doom and glory of knowing who you are. *Life Magazine.*

Bogel, A. (n.d.). 16 Books that are better together: 8 terrific novels paired with 8 illuminating nonfiction picks to elevate your reading experience. *Modern Mrs Darcy.*

Booth, W. C. (1988). *The company we keep: An ethics of fiction* (1st ed.). University of California Press.

Bristow, N. K., Johnston, A., Linenthal, E. T., Pfeifer, M. J., Shine, J., & Williams, K. E. (2015, May). Trauma and trigger warnings in the history classroom: A roundtable discussion. Retrieved from https://www .oah .org/tah/

issues/2015/may/trauma -and -trigger -warnings -in -the -history-classroom/

Brooklyn Museum. (2017) The legacy of lynching: Confronting racial terror in America. Retrieved from https://www.brooklynmuseum.org/exhibitions/legacy_of_lynchin

Cotter, B. J. (2018, May 20). Teacher's dilemma: Should author's bad behavior ban the book? *The Day.*

Cotter, B. J. (2020, February 8). Ethnic litmus test only divides us further. *Providence Journal.*

Cummins, J. (2019). *American dirt.* Flatiron Books.

Dewey, J. (1997). *Experience and education.* Free Press.

#DisruptTexts. (n.d.). #DisruptTexts. https://disrupttexts.org/

Filipovic, J. (2014, March 5). We've gone too far with "trigger warnings." *The Guardian.*

Gordimer, N. (2001, December 5). *Witness: The inward testimony.* Nobel Centennial Symposia.

Graff, G. (1991). Teach the conflicts. In D. Gless & B. Herrnstein Smith (Eds.), *The politics of liberal education* (pp. 57–74). Duke University Press.

Gurba, M. (2019, December 12). Pendeja, you ain't Steinbeck: My bronca with fake-ass social justice literature. *Tropics of Meta.*

Hannah, L. (n.d.). Book trigger list. *Autism, Mental Health, Books & Simple Living.*

hooks, b. (1994). *Teaching to transgress: Education as a practice of freedom.* Routledge.

Hoover, J. (2021, July 9). Critical race theory hysteria overshadows the importance of teaching kids about racism. *Vox.*

Jacobs, A. (2020). *Breaking bread with the dead.* Penguin Press.

Jarrett, C. (2019, December 19). Trigger warnings don't help people cope with distressing material. *The Wire.*

Jones, P. J., Bellet, B. W., & McNally, R. J. (2020, June 1). Helping or harming? The effect of trigger warnings on individuals with trauma histories. Retrieved from *Clinical Psychological Science.* Sagepub.com

Kafka, F. (1959). *Letters to family, friends, and editors.* Schocken Books.

Kenney, M. (2014). Teaching the n-word. *Rethinking Schools, 29*(1).

Khalid, A., & Snyder, J. A. (2021). The data is in— Trigger warnings don't work. *The Chronicle of Higher Education.*

Kidd, D. C., & Castano, E. (2013). Reading literary fiction improves theory of mind. *Science, 342*(6156), 377–380.

Lee, H. (1960, July 11). *To kill a mockingbird.* Harper Collins.

Lone Star. (2021, September 27). *What is cancel culture?* Research guides, Lone Star College.

Mishan, L. (2020, December 3). The long and tortured history of cancel culture. *New York Times Style Magazine.*

Orwell, G. (1946). Why I write: Essays and other works. Retrieved from https://www.orwellfoundation.com/the-orwell-foundation/orwell/essays-and-other-works/why-i-write/

Penguin Classroom. (n.d.). #DisruptTexts in your classroom with these 8 texts! https://penguinclassroom.com/books/disrupt-texts-in-your-classroom-educator-guide/

Perry Jr., W. G. (1970). *Forms of intellectual and ethical development in the college years: A scheme*. Holt, Rinehart, and Winston.

Pineda, D. (2020, November 12). In Burbank schools, a book-banning debate over how to teach antiracism. *Los Angeles Times*.

Porter, R. (2019, December 19). This is not a drill: It's time to #cancel JK Rowling. *Rori Porter*.

Prior, K. S. (2013, June 21). How reading makes us more human. *The Atlantic*.

Richards, I. A. (1929). *Practical criticism*. Harcourt, Brace & World.

Rosenblatt, L. M. (1938). *Literature as exploration*. D. Appleton-Century Co.

Rosenfield, K. (2017, August 7). The toxic drama on YA Twitter. *New York Magazine*.

Rueb, E. S., & Taylor, D. B. (2019, October 31). Obama on call-out culture: "That's not activism." *New York Times*.

Sawchuk, S. (2021, May 18). What is critical race theory, and why is it under attack? *Education Week*.

Shapiro, L. (2021, January 4). Blurbed to death. *New York Magazine*.

Sims Bishop, R. (1990). Mirrors, windows, and sliding glass doors. In *Perspectives: Choosing and Using Books for the Classroom* (3rd ed., Vol. 6).

Singal, J. (2019, January 31). How a Twitter mob derailed an immigrant female author's budding career. *Tablet*.

Stallworth, B. J., & Gibbons, L. C. (2012). What's on the list . . . now? A survey of book-length works taught in secondary schools. *English Leadership Quarterly, 34*(3), 2–3.

Steinbeck, J. (1939). *The grapes of wrath*. Viking Press-James Lloyd.

Stevens, H. (2021, March 9). What a Woody Allen reckoning can teach us about Lincoln statues, Dr. Seuss and the British royal family. *Chicago Tribune*.

Stone, D. (2014, September 15). Why trigger warnings don't work. *Stir*.

Torres, C. (2019, October 1). Why I'm rethinking teaching Shakespeare in my English classroom. *Education Week*.

University Health Service-University of Wisconsin Madison Retrieved from: https://www.uhs.wisc.edu/prevention/violence-prevention/faculty-staff-vp-resources/

University of Michigan. (2021). An introduction to content warnings and trigger warnings. Retrieved from https://sites.lsa.umich.edu/inclusive-teaching-sandbox/wp-content/uploads/sites/853/2021/02/An-Introduction-to-Content-Warnings-and-Trigger-Warnings-Draft.pdf

University of Waterloo. (n.d.). *Trigger warnings*. Centre for Teaching Excellence.

Verges, J. (2020, December 22). Sibley High School pulls two books from English classes, citing complaints. *Twin Cities Pioneer Press*.

Waldman, K. (2019, March 21). In Y.A., where is the line between criticism and cancel culture? *The New Yorker.*

Why we oppose morals clauses in book contracts. (2019, January 24). *The Authors Guild.*

Winterich, J. A. (2015, October 9). Trigger or not, warnings matter. *Inside Higher Ed.*

Yar, S., & Bromwich, J. E. (2019, October 31). Tales from the teenage cancel culture. *New York Times.*

Zinn Education Project. (2021, August 20). Teachers refuse to lie to students. *Zinn Education Project.*

INDEX

ABOUT THE AUTHOR

Deborah Appleman is the Hollis L. Caswell Professor of Educational Studies at Carleton College. Since 2007, she has taught language, literature, and creative writing courses at a high-security prison for men in the Upper Midwest, which formed the focus of her recent book, *Words No Bars Can Old: Literacy Learning in Prison.*

Professor Appleman taught high school English for nine years before receiving her doctorate from the University of Minnesota. She was also a visiting professor at Syracuse University and at the University of California, Berkeley. She is the author of *Critical Encounters in Secondary English: Teaching Literary Theory to Adolescents, Third Edition* (winner of the Richard A. Meade Award); *Adolescent Literacy and the Teaching of Reading; Adolescent Literacies: A Handbook of Practice-Based Research* (editor); *Teaching Literature to Adolescents, Third Edition* (with Richard Beach, Bob Fecho, and Rob Simon); *Reading for Themselves: How to Transform Adolescents into Lifelong Readers Through Out-of-Class Book Clubs; Uncommon Core; Reading Better, Reading Smarter*; and coeditor of *Braided Lives: An Anthology of Multicultural American Writing.*